Other books by J. Cameron Fraser:

Thandabantu: The Man Who Loved the People

God Is Always Good: Cassidy's Story
(with Sonya M. Taekema)

A Personal Appreciation of D. A. Macfarlane

Developments in Biblical Counseling

LEARNING FROM LORD MACKAY:

Life and Work in Two Kingdoms

J. Cameron Fraser

Foreword by Sinclair B. Ferguson

SoS-Books

Lethbridge, Alberta, Canada

Learning from Lord Mackay:
Life and Work in Two Kingdoms

Except where noted, biblical references are from the King James Version. Reference to the ESV is from The Holy Bible, English Standard Version, copyright © 2001 by Crossway Bibles, a publishing ministry of Good News Publishers. Used by permission. All rights reserved.

Printed in the United States of America

Cataloguing data available from Library and Archives Canada

Fraser, J. Cameron (John Cameron), 1954-
Learning from Lord Mackay:
Life and Work in Two Kingdoms

ISBN:978-0-9959953-0-7(hardcover)

ISBN:978-0-9959953-1-4 (paperback)

ISBN:978-0-9959953-2-1 (ebook)

Design and formatting by Ruth May and The Warwick Printing Co. Ltd., Lethbridge, Alberta

Photographs not otherwise acknowledged are public domain.

Cover photo: Lord Mackay sitting on the Woolsack, the seat of the Lord Speaker in the House of Lords. Courtesy of Lord Mackay, from a print of an original photograph in Alastair Bruce, *Keepers of the Kingdom: The Ancient Offices of Britain* (London: Weidenfield and Nicolson 1999). Photograph by Mark Cator.

To order additional copies, visit:
www.SoS-Books.com

No. 6, Professional Building
740 4 Ave S, Lethbridge, AB T1J 0N9 Canada

To James Mackay, in appreciation,
for his 90th birthday

Contents

Foreword

IT IS A PRIVILEGE TO INTRODUCE *Learning from Lord Mackay*. There is no Scotsman, indeed no British person in public life whom I admire more. The sight of his face, or the sound of his voice, on television or radio have always been an immediate encouragement to me. The calm demeanour, the modest but assured bearing, the clear and precise speech, coloured by the lilt of a gentle Scottish accent, the superb intelligence, the ability to think clearly and in a way that gets to the heart of the matter, the way he articulates his views with grace, the respect for others—all these qualities and more lift the spirit.

I suspect this impressiveness is noticed even by those who never pause to enquire what it is that ultimately has made Lord Mackay both the man and the public servant he has been. But the reason is not hidden. It is that his life has been consistently undergirded by his Christian faith, his devotion to Christ, and the resulting desire to "do justice, love mercy, and to walk humbly with his God." There is no bombast here, no demeaning of others, only an adorning of the Christian faith. I have sometimes wondered, "Was Daniel a man like this? Is this why he was able to negotiate life in the Babylonian Empire?" For Lord Mackay has encouraged me to believe that in what is now widely spoken of as a post-Christian society, it is still possible to "sing the Lord's song in a strange land." He not only possesses extraordinary intellectual equipment; he has also modelled for us the importance, and the impact, of genuine Christian character.

It may be helpful for North American readers to know that Lord Mackay is a *Law* Lord, that is his title relates to the eminent positions in the judiciary to which Prime Minister Margaret Thatcher appointed him—first from 1979 until 1984 in Scotland's highest legal office as Lord Advocate, and then from 1987-1997 as Lord High Chancellor of Great Britain. The dignity of the latter Office of State is perhaps best communicated by saying that its origins lie in the Middle Ages, it includes a seat in the Cabinet and, in Lord Mackay's day, involved serving as the presiding officer in the House of Lords. In addition, the order of precedence in the United Kingdom is such that the Lord Chancellor outranks even the Prime Minister! For an entire decade, he sat in the British Cabinet and at the same time was responsible in that position for maintaining the absolute independence of the Judiciary. Surely a task requiring not only wisdom but tact!

No one could doubt that Lord Mackay attained the high honour of these positions on the basis of great personal ability and distinction. One does not receive honorary doctorates at the rate of one per year between 1983 and 2000 without peer-recognition of unusual ability. And only someone of distinction would be granted fellowships in as diverse academies as (among others), the International

Academy of Trial Lawyers, the American College of Trial Lawyers, the Chartered Institute of Taxation, Trinity College and Girton College in the University of Cambridge, and Royal Colleges of Surgeons, the Royal College of Physicians (both of Edinburgh) and even the Royal College of Obstetricians and Gynaecologists!

What is perhaps most impressive of all, however, is the manner in which both ability and distinction rest lightly on Lord Mackay's shoulders. When he takes his place, with Lady Mackay, among God's people in worship and prayer, fellow-Christians with whom he rubs shoulders sense that he comes with them as a child to his heavenly Father, in need of the grace of Christ the Saviour, desiring to live in the strength of the Spirit. In this sense, without seeking to be hagiographical, for many of us, his fellow Scots, he has modelled in a most attractive and engaging way the power of Paul's words: "What do you have that you did not receive? If then you received it, why do you boast as if you did not receive it?" (1 Cor. 4:7, ESV). Lord Mackay reminds me of Chaucer's famous description of the Knight in *The Canterbury Tales*—if "Lord" may be substituted here for (the lower rank of) Knight:

> He was very wise
> And of temper as meekly as a maid.
> He never yet had any vileness said,
> In all his life, to whatsoever wight [person].
> He was a truly perfect, noble knight.

Some years ago, a friend who had been part of the legal team in a court case presided over by Lord Mackay related an experience that illustrates a quality that is evident even in passing conversation. Following his "summing up" of the case, the legal teams of both parties had walked out of court together. One of the lawyers representing "the opposition" turned to my friend and said, "Now at last we understand what the legal issues in this case really are!" As Cameron Fraser's cameo portrait makes clear, this remarkable intellectual gift of grasping all the facts and seeing to the heart of an issue, coupled with the wisdom to know what to do with that knowledge, have been woven into a character that has been shaped by God's grace. Such a combination underlines it, not only in studying the Bible, but in the whole of the life that Christians are called to love the Lord not only with all our heart, soul, and strength, but also with our mind. And in doing this as an interpreter and applier of the law of the land, Lord Mackay has sought simultaneously to love his neighbour as himself. Even those to whom he has handed down sentences are made as the image of God. Cameron records testimony to this in the pages that follow.

The political world which Lord Mackay entered is by no means an easy one to negotiate as a Christian. There are party political pressures, as well as social pressures. In addition, for a Christian there can be additional pressures. Sometimes they come from opponents of the Christian faith. Illogically non-Christian presuppositions are allowed to influence political decisions whereas Christian ones are regarded as illegitimately prejudicial! But unfortunately, Christians in public service may also face "friendly-fire" from fellow-believers who do not always grasp that politics is the art of the possible (or that in our law courts the accused is both innocent in law until proved guilty, and entitled to the best defence under the law!). Christians in public office are not able to turn a fallen world order into a perfect one. And therein lies a problem for public servants—for not all Christians understand this, sometimes with unhappy results.

With these and similar issues Lord Mackay has had to deal. He has done so with great dignity as well as articulating his views with clarity. Has he always been right? It is one of the merits of Cameron's tribute that these pages not only introduce us to Lord Mackay but also stimulate that question and will, at the very least, cause us to pause and pray for wisdom for those Christians who seek to render to Caesar what belongs to him while rendering to God what belongs to him.

Cameron brings his own gifts to this pen portrait. He himself possesses an able mind. But in addition, as will become clear, Lord Mackay is someone who has simply been "there" during the whole of his life, and his affection for him is patent. From a purely selfish point of view I wish that he might have been able to persuade him to appoint him as "official biographer" and write a much longer book—

perhaps with some such title as *Lord Mackay of Clashfern—A Noble Life*. But this is not in any sense to detract from the interest and value of *Learning from Lord Mackay*. Rather it is an expression of esteem for the subject of these pages and appreciation of what Cameron Fraser has done. It is only natural that admirers wish to know much more about the person they admire!

I hope that these pages will serve as an attractive and thought-provoking introduction to Lord Mackay of Clashfern. More than that—(and this, I suspect, would give him much pleasure)—I hope they may stimulate a young man or woman to think, "Perhaps I can serve God in the way Lord Mackay of Clashfern has done."

Sinclair B. Ferguson, Ph.D.

Preface

THE SUBJECT PROFILED IN THIS BRIEF WORK is well-known in legal circles around the world. He has shared a platform with evangelist Billy Graham and chaired a Luis Palau crusade. He counted the late John Stott as a close friend. Yet he is not as well-known among Christians in general outside of the United Kingdom. The purpose of this essay is, in part, to rectify this. It is also to share his insights, especially with evangelical Christians involved in the American political process and with those involved in the current (largely American) "two kingdoms" controversy.

Some of what is written here originated as an article in the Canadian-based *Haddington House Journal* (*HHJ*, 2014). The title, "A British Christian in Public Office," was intentional. There are aspects of Lord Mackay's life and work that are typically British as well as Christian (not that the two designations are synonymous!) But for both of these reasons, I believe he may have something to teach fellow believers in other parts of the world, especially in the world's leading democracy in the age of Trump. (I am aware that this, and a few other references, will soon become dated, but I trust the main body of the essay will have abiding relevance.) Lord Mackay was a frequent visitor to the United States throughout his career and, in 1990, became an honorary member of the American College of Trial Lawyers.

A much shorter version of the *HHJ* article appeared in the *Christian Courier* (September 8, 2014). The editor chose the title, "Learning from Lord Mackay," and I have borrowed it for the title of this essay.

The first chapter is mostly from a substantially abbreviated version of another *HHJ* article, "Reformed Developments in Two Kingdoms Doctrine" (2017). I am grateful to Dr. Jack C. Whytock, editor of the *HHJ*, and to Angela Reitsma Bick, editor of the *Christian Courier*, for permission to use material that originally appeared in their publications. Thanks also to:

- James Hamilton, Research Principal at the Signet Library in Edinburgh, for permission to quote from "Lord Mackay of Clashfern, From the Highlands to High Office," and "From the Court Room to the Cabinet Room": Interview with Robert Pirrie in *Signet Magazine: The Magazine of the Writers to Her Majesty's Signet,* The WS Society, Edinburgh, Parts 1 and 2, July 2012, February 2013, Issues 3 & 4.

- Annie Pinder, the Office Manager of Parliamentary Archives, Houses of Parliament, London, UK for help with the terms and conditions of reprinting a speech by Lord Mackay from Hansard archives.

- Anna Wheeler for permission to reprint "Does Establishment Have a Future? From *Theos: Clear thinking on religion and society*, 13th May, 2013.

- John Macleod, for permission to use material from his book, *No Great Mischief if You Fall: The Highland Experience* (Edinburgh: Mainstream Publishing Co., 1994).

- Redeemer City to City and Timothy J. Keller for permission to use material from Timothy Keller, *Center Church* (Zondervan, 2012).

- Sally Maciver, Administrator, Residential, for permission to use a photograph from the Saville, Edinburgh website http://www.rightmoveread the. co.uk/property-for-sale/property-49682362.htm.

Sinclair Ferguson not only wrote the gracious foreword, but took on the role of editor, suggesting several improvements to the manuscript. My wife's editing skills were also put to good use, and I am grateful to Bob Derrik, John Frame, James Fraser, Roderick Gray, Ken Stewart, David VanDrunen, and Nicol Warn for reading and critiquing all or part of the manuscript. Lord Mackay also read and approved the manuscript, making some relatively minor but important revisions.

The foreword provides a wonderful introduction to Lord Mackay. If readers were to read only that, part of my goal would be realised in terms of introducing him to a wider audience. I identify especially with the first paragraph. After several months of research on Lord Mackay's public record, as I stressed over what to include or not, I watched a televised interview that had the precise effect on me that Sinclair describes so eloquently.

I am most grateful to Lord and Lady Mackay for their kind hospitality and cooperation in bygone days as well as more recently. Lady Mackay in particular has the unique gift of making visitors to her lovely home feel as if they are more important than she is; that she is the one privileged to be entertaining them. She is, in her husband's words, "absolutely extraordinary."

Lord Mackay has declined requests for biographies or an autobiography. He has no scores to settle and no interest in self-promotion. I am privileged that he has agreed (with some initial reluctance), to be profiled here on the understanding that my role is that of an essayist and not a biographer.

I am a proud Canadian Scot who grew up in Scotland and have known James and Bett Mackay since my youth. I try not to inject myself too much into the story, but I avoid literary formalities like "the author" or "the present writer." In typically Canadian fashion, I use British spelling, except when quoting from an American source and American punctuation, except when quoting from a British source. American punctuation values appearance over strict grammatical accuracy, meaning that when a quotation appears within a sentence the punctuation mark is within rather than outside of the quotation marks, as per the *Chicago Manual of Style*.

Finally, it seems appropriate to note that this book is being published in the same year as the 500th anniversary of the Protestant Reformation. Besides references to Luther and Calvin, I would hope that what follows bears some witness to the abiding relevance of Reformation principles.

1
Introducing Two Kingdoms

Andrew Melville (1545-1622)

SIR, AS DIVERS TIMES BEFORE, so now again, I must tell you, there are two Kings and two Kingdoms in Scotland: there is Christ Jesus the King, and his Kingdom the Kirk, whose subject King James the Sixth is, and of whose kingdom not a king, nor a lord, nor a head, but a member!"[1] So spoke Andrew Melville (1545-1622) to King James VI of Scotland, soon to become James I of England and Ireland following the

---

[1] Translated into modern English in Elizabeth Whitley, *The Two Kingdoms* (Edinburgh: The Scottish Reformation Society, 1977), 26.

union of the Scottish and English crowns in 1603. Melville's point was to affirm the independence of the Church of Scotland from state control, a principle for which many of the Scottish Covenanters would later give their lives.[2] As the late G. N. M. Collins (1901-89) wrote in the foreword to Elizabeth Whitley's *The Two Kingdoms,* Melville "was enunciating no new principle of Church and State relations, but merely reasserting one which had been basic to the Scottish Reformation, and which inhered in the concordat between Church and State relating to the establishment of the Reformed Church in Scotland."[3]

The language of two kingdoms suggests the influence of Martin Luther (1483-1546) and Lutheranism, with whom the doctrine is most commonly associated. Luther taught that since God rules over the whole world, he does so in two ways. Earthly kingdoms are ruled through secular and religious powers by the enforcement of law, whereas members of the heavenly or spiritual kingdom of God are governed by the gospel of grace.[4] Christians live in and may serve both kingdoms, although a popular saying attributed to Luther is that a competent unbeliever ("Turk") as an earthly governor is preferable to an incompetent believer. It

2   For a popular history of the Covenanters, see the above reference. A more extensive treatment can be found in Alexander Smellie, *Men of the Covenant: The Story of the Scottish Church in the Years of the Persecution* (London, Andrew Melrose, 1908). See also James Barr, *The Scottish Covenanters* (Glasgow: John Smith & Son, 1946).
3   G. N. M. Collins, Foreword to Elizabeth Whitley, op. cit, v.
4   For a helpful discussion and defence of Luther's two kingdoms doctrine, see inter alia, Anders Nygren, "Luther's Doctrine of the Two Kingdoms," in *Journal of Lutheran Ethics*, Vol.2, Issue 8, *http://www.elca.org/JLE/Articles/931.*

is difficult to find actual documentation for this, but it does sound like something Luther might have said!

Martin Luther (1483-1546)
Portrait by
Lucas Cranach the Elder 1529

Although there was early Lutheran influence in the Scottish Reformation, the predominant influence on its leading reformer John Knox (1514-72) and his successor Andrew Melville came from John Calvin (1509-64), who wrote of a distinction between the "spiritual" and "civil" kingdom.[5] He went on to say, "Yet this distinction does not lead us to consider the whole nature of government a thing polluted, which has nothing to do with Christian men."[6] He called "fanatical" the view that as members of the spiritual kingdom of God, believers have no responsibility to earthly powers. This was an allusion to the Anabaptists of his day (also opposed by Luther) who understood Jesus to

---

5   John Calvin, *Institutes of the Christian Religion*, 3 vols., trans. Henry Beveridge (Edinburgh: Calvin Translation Society, 1845), 3.19.15. It should be noted that two kingdoms doctrine is broader in its scope than church-state relations, but this is what our primary focus will be here.
6   Ibid., 4.20.11.

teach that civil government belongs to this world and that Christians as citizens of the kingdom of God should not hold office or actively serve earthly governments, to whom they are obliged only to offer passive non-resistance (Matthew 22:21, John 18:36; cf. Romans 13:1-7).

John Calvin (1509-64)
Portrait attributed to Hans Holbein the Younger

Calvin believed that "civil government is necessary to preserve outward order and piety in the age before Christ's return." He argued that civil government "is to enforce the first table of the law, as well as the second." Calvin "did not believe civil government was obligated to conform slavishly to the civil laws and penalties in the Torah. But he did believe government was to be concerned with the preservation of outward piety, in addition to justice." He insisted that government "had the duty of 'rightly establishing religion' (4.20.3) in order that God might be honored, the public protected from scandal, and people who did not yet believe the gospel or accept the law might be exposed to its proclamation."[7]

This view found expression in various Reformed confessions, such as the *Belgic Confession* (1561) and the *Westminster Confession of Faith* (1647). The latter confession, in its original wording, strikes Calvin's balance between the roles of the two kingdoms:

> The civil magistrate may not assume to himself the administration of the Word and sacraments, or the power of the keys of the kingdom of heaven: yet he hath authority, and it is his duty, to take order, that unity and peace be preserved in the Church, that the truth of God be kept pure and entire; that all blasphemies and heresies be suppressed; all corruptions and abuses in worship and discipline prevented or reformed; and all the ordinances of God duly settled, administered, and observed. For the better effecting whereof, he hath power to call synods, to be present at them, and to provide that whatsoever is transacted in them be according to the mind of God.[8]

When the Presbyterian Church in the United States was formed in 1788, it revised this paragraph so that it now reads:

---

7   Matthew Tuininga, "The Two Kingdoms Doctrine, Part Two: John Calvin," http://www.reformation21.org/articles/the-two-kingdoms-doctrine-part-two-john-calvin.phpn, October 2012.

8   *The Westminster Confession of Faith and Larger and Shorter Catechism* (Glasgow: Free Presbyterian Publications, 1970), Chapter XXIII, paragraph III.

Civil magistrates may not assume to themselves the administration of the Word and sacraments; or the power of the keys of the kingdom of heaven; or, in the least, interfere in matters of faith. Yet, as nursing fathers, it is the duty of civil magistrates to protect the church of our common Lord, without giving the preference to any denomination of Christians above the rest, in such a manner that all ecclesiastical persons whatever shall enjoy the full, free, and unquestioned liberty of discharging every part of their sacred functions, without violence or danger. And, as Jesus Christ hath appointed a regular government and discipline in his church, no law of any commonwealth should interfere with, let, or hinder, the due exercise thereof, among the voluntary members of any denomination of Christians, according to their own profession and belief. It is the duty of civil magistrates to protect the person and good name of all their people, in such an effectual manner as that no person be suffered, either upon pretence of religion or of infidelity, to offer any indignity, violence, abuse, or injury to any other person whatsoever: and to take order, that all religious and ecclesiastical assemblies be held without molestation or disturbance.[9]

---

9   *The Westminster Confession of Faith and Catechisms As Adopted by the Presbyterian Church in America* (copyright 2005, 2007 by the Orthodox Presbyterian Church) Chapter 23, paragraph 3. The late Greg Bahnsen, author of *Theonomy in Christian Ethics*, and a principal leader in the movement known as Theonomy or Christian Reconstruction, suggested

This change predated and anticipated the First Amendment to the United States' Constitution (1791) which states in part, "Congress shall make no law respecting an establishment of religion, or prohibiting the free exercise thereof..." It has also been defended on historical and biblical grounds.[10]

The Pilgrim Fathers who first colonised New England were fleeing persecution by the established Church of England. One practical result of this was the exclusion of clergy from political office in New England. At the same time, the pilgrims "held to the belief, common in their day, that the establishment of religion by civil law was both right and necessary." Their goal was "to establish in the New World a branch of the Church of England, but without the alleged corruptions and false practices which they deplored so deeply in the Church of the mother country."[11]

that this change is a clarification rather than a correction. He also believed that the Westminster divines taught that the civil penalties of the Mosaic law were still in effect. Sinclair Ferguson demonstrates that this was not the case, although he does concede that "there may be common ground in practice between the Confession's teaching and theonomy" [Sinclair B. Ferguson, "An Assembly of Theonomists? The Teaching of the Westminster Divines on the Law of God" in William Barker, W. Robert Godfrey eds., *Theonomy: A Reformed Critique* (Grand Rapids, MI: Zondervan, 1990), 347.] It is certainly the case that the majority of Puritans, and Calvin before them, taught that the first table of the moral law should be enforced by the civil magistrate and they also believed in capital punishment for offenses other than murder. This was not because they thought the entire Mosaic law should be imposed on modern nations, but because they applied the principle of "general equity," meaning the application of general principles to the contemporary situation. Different Puritans, including those who composed the Westminster Confession, applied those principles differently.

10 See, for instance, Charles Hodge's "The Relation of Church and State," first published in the *Princeton Review* (1863) and reprinted in Hodge's *The Church and Its Polity* (London: Thomas Nelson and Sons, 1879), 106-18.

11 J. Marcellus Kik, *Church and State: The Story of Two Kingdoms* (New York:

The Church of England was likewise the established church of Virginia. It was against this background that the so-called "establishment clause" of the First Amendment was adopted, to enshrine universal liberty of conscience for religious and ecclesiastical minorities.[12]

The well-known words of the United States' Declaration of Independence (1776) that all men are created equal and are endowed by their Creator with certain inalienable rights, including life, liberty and the pursuit of happiness, are widely considered to be an adaptation of language used by the English philosopher John Locke (1632-1704). Francis Schaeffer (1912-84) in *A Christian Manifesto* asserts that Locke had secularised and drawn heavily from the Scottish divine Samuel Rutherford's (1600-61) classic work, *Lex Rex* (1644).[13] Written in defence of the Scottish Covenanters against the imposition of the divine right of kings,[14] *Lex Rex* argued that, rather than the king being above the law, he was subject to it. All civil power is derived from God. Power is a birthright of the people from whom the king borrows. If the king abuses that power by

Thomas Nelson & Sons, 1963), 108.

12 For a helpful overview of the development of religious liberty in the colonies, leading up to the "establishment clause" and its implications, see Mark A. Noll, *The Old Religion in a New World: The History of North American Christianity* (Eerdmans, 2002), chapter 4, "The Separation of Church and State," 72-94.

13 Francis A. Schaeffer, *A Christian Manifesto* (Westchester, Illinois: Crossway Books, 1981, revised 1982), 32. Schaeffer's inference that the authors of the American Constitution were thereby influenced by Rutherford's Christian principles is disputed by several scholars of American history.

14 *Lex Rex* was written in response to a 1644 work by John Maxwell, onetime Bishop of Ross, *The Sacred and Royal Prerogative of Christian Kings*, defending absolute monarchy and the divine right of kings.

oppressing the people, they are entitled to recover it by means of armed revolution.

There are certainly echoes of this in the Declaration of Independence and the Constitution of the United States. John Macleod, in his 1938 lectures at Westminster Seminary in Philadelphia, notes that Rutherford's influence, and that of others who followed him, "told directly through

Samuel Rutherford (c.1600-61)

the teaching of John Witherspoon[15]... and indirectly through the teaching of John Locke.... Jefferson was of this school."[16] However, Rutherford also wrote in *Lex Rex* that "God is the author of civil laws and government, and his intention is therein the external peace, and quiet life, and godliness of

15 Witherspoon (1723-94) was President of what is now Princeton University (1768-94), a Presbyterian minister who immigrated from Scotland, and the only clergyman to sign the Declaration of Independence.
16 John Macleod, *Scottish Theology: In relation to Church History* (Edinburgh: The Knox Press and The Banner of Truth Trust, 1974 reprint), 72.

his church and people, and that all judges, according to their places, be nurse-fathers to the church (Isa 49:23)."[17] He was a commissioner to the Westminster Assembly and agreed with the teaching of its resulting *Confession of Faith* that the civil magistrate had the authority and duty to suppress "all blasphemies and heresies." He did not envision a situation where equal rights were granted to people of all faiths and none.

Thus, while Calvin's followers, in both the old world and the early days of the new world in America, held to a form of what came to be known as "two kingdoms doctrine," with separate and limited jurisdictions for church and state, they also believed that these institutions were mutually interdependent expressions of Christ's lordship. The establishment of national churches, opposed by the Constitution of the United States and the American revisions to the *Westminster Confession of Faith,* was the norm. The situation today is much different in what are now Great Britain and the United States of America, as in the Western world generally, where pluralism and secular values, often hostile to Christian principles, hold sway. How is a Christian in the tradition of the *Westminster Confession* to conduct himself in such a context? This essay offers one example in the person of Lord James Mackay of Clashfern, at one time Britain's Lord Chancellor.

---

17   Samuel Rutherford, *Lex Rex, or The Law and the Prince: A Dispute for the Just Prerogative of King and People* (Originally published 1644, reprinted by Sprinkle Publications, 1980), 105.

The office of Lord Chancellor is unique to the British system of government. It has no parallel in American politics or, for that matter, in those of commonwealth countries such as Australia or Canada. However, as stated in the preface, I believe that there are lessons to be learned from Lord Mackay that are of universal application. These are found in Chapter 3. I shall also attempt to locate Lord Mackay in relation to contemporary debates (mainly in the United States) on the value or otherwise of "two kingdoms doctrine" (Chapter 4).

2
Introducing Lord Mackay: Life and Work

IN 2012, THE BRITISH GOVERNMENT of the day introduced changes to the Child Support Agency (CSA) such that, under a new Child Maintenance Service, a non-resident parent — the one not taking care of the children — would be given the opportunity to make child support payments directly to the parent providing care rather than having them collected by the CSA. If the payments were not maintained regularly, the government would charge the parent providing care for collecting the money on their behalf. On January 29, 2012, a young single mother by the name of Emily blogged as follows:

> On Wednesday night, the Coalition Government suffered its biggest defeat in the House of Lords since it was elected. It was a landslide: 270 over 128. The vote was for an amendment to the planned CSA charges, tabled by Lord Mackay of Clashfern.
>
> Last year, I <u>wrote</u> and <u>wrote</u> and <u>wrote</u> about the Government's plans.... I didn't just write about it on my blog: I wrote to my MP and I wrote to the Consultation, as well as

speaking to them on the phone.... No one paid any attention...

Then along came Lord Mackay of Clashfern, leading a wonderful revolt and talking absolute sense...

When I watched him speaking in the House of Lords... I cried. Finally, a Conservative... who wants fairness, a man who understands the reality of thousands of single parents. I never thought I would want to hug a Tory peer.

I can't give Lord Mackay of Clashfern a hug, but I am going to write him a thank you letter — and I hope others who helped campaign against these charges will have the time to do the same.[1]

A subsequent comment (Feb 13, 2012) revealed, "I emailed him and he wrote back to me the next morning — and signed it 'James'. He's got to be the best Tory peer going. Alas, the MPs didn't take any notice and ignored him anyway."[2]

Heart-warming comments of this nature are typical of those who have seen and heard Lord Mackay in action. His vote against his own political party is also typical of his commitment to doing what he believes to be right,

---

1 "Thanks, Lord Mackay of Clashfern." Posted by Emily on Jan 29, 2012 in Single Parent Stuff, http://myshittytwenties.co.uk/2012/01/29/thanks-lord-mackay-of-clashfern.

2 For the distinction between Members of Parliament (MPs) and peers in the House of Lords, see later.

regardless of political considerations. Still active, now in his tenth decade, Mackay frequently flies to London from his Scottish Highland home of Inverness to speak and vote in the House of Lords on matters of socio-ethical significance. The values he espouses are ones he learned in his religiously devout upbringing.

Early Life and Career

James Peter Hymers Mackay (commonly known to friends as James Peter), was born in July 1927, in Edinburgh, the Scottish capital. His father came from the remote Highland home of Clashfern in west Sutherland, and had worked as a porter/signalman for the Caledonian Railway Company. James's mother was originally from Halkirk, Caithness, in the very far north of Scotland. His parents married late in life, his mother having been previously widowed, and James was an only son. A popularly circulated story has a pious old woman meeting the couple after they had been married and childless for some years. She assured them that they would yet have a son who would "rise high in goodness and ability."[3]

James's father was an active elder in the local congregation of the Free Presbyterian Church of Scotland, and it was in this theologically conservative denomination that James was nurtured spiritually, leading to his own profession of faith as a young man. He would later become

---

3   See John Macleod, *No Great Mischief If You Fall: The Highland Experience* (Edinburgh: Mainstream Publishing Company, 1993), 91. Macleod adds "But stories of this sort are so common in the Highlands, and so frequently retrospective that perhaps we should not believe this."

an elder himself, and served the denomination as legal adviser and assistant clerk of Synod for a number of years.

As a young boy, James won a scholarship to George Heriot's, an elite school in Edinburgh. School holidays were spent on the Caithness farm of a widowed uncle and his seven children, thus establishing a life-long connection with the north of Scotland and its simpler life-style. James went on to study mathematics and natural philosophy (physics) at the University of Edinburgh, receiving a joint M.A. in 1948. He was awarded a scholarship to Trinity College, Cambridge, but first there was the matter of national service. At the Joint Recruiting Office, he was told that there was a shortage of lecturers in mathematics and he should satisfy his national service obligations by filling one of the university vacancies in Scotland. This led to two years of teaching at the University of St. Andrews before pursuing further studies at Cambridge University, from which he graduated in 1952.

One unintended consequence of James's time at Cambridge was the decision that his future lay not in academic mathematics but in law. At Trinity College he met Michael Atiyah, who was to become one of the leading mathematicians in the world and winner (in 2004) of the Abel Prize, often described as "the mathematician's Nobel Prize." James recalls, "He was a good friend of mine, but when I saw his capabilities I realised that my role wasn't in academic mathematics for the rest of my life." His mother

James Mackay's parents as he remembers them, c. 1940

had passed away and his father was on his own in Edinburgh, so James returned there. He "had done all the mathematics that Edinburgh University had to offer... and thought [he'd] like to do law and never regretted that decision."[4]

James received an LL.B. (with distinction) in 1955. In that same year, he was elected to the Faculty of Advocates (the Scottish Bar). He had a "terrific" time and found that his natural shyness left him in the cut and thrust of legal debates. In 1963, as a junior counsel he represented the Duke of Argyll in a sensational divorce case that made

---

4   "Lord Mackay of Clashfern, Part 1: From the Highlands to High Office." Interview with Robert Pirrie in *Signet Magazine: The Magazine of the Writers to Her Majesty's Signet*, July 2012-Issue 3:19.

newspaper headlines. This was followed by several less prominent divorce cases that gave him experience with family law and the bitterness of divorce, an experience that was to stand him in good stead in later years when, as Britain's Lord Chancellor, he introduced divorce reform legislation.

A decade after being called to the Bar, James Mackay "took silk," becoming a Queen's Counsel. He was Sheriff Principal for Renfrew and Argyle from 1972 to 1974. In 1973, he became Vice-Dean of the Faculty of Advocates, and from 1976 to 1979 served as its Dean, making him the leader of the Scottish Bar.

Family Life in Edinburgh

In 1958 James married a distant cousin, Elizabeth (Bett) Hymers, and together they had a son and two daughters. Their son James is a genetic oncologist in London. The younger daughter Ruth is Managing Director of a veterinary practice in Lancashire. The middle child Elizabeth (Liz) graduated in Business Studies from Herriot-Watt University in Edinburgh. She married James Campbell, a frequent visitor to the Mackay home when he was a boarder at George Watson's School. Campbell is now Chief Executive of Blythswood Care, a Christian charity based in the Scottish Highlands, to whose ministry his father-in-law has contributed his influence from time to time as its patron.[5]

---

5   Blythswood's remarkable development from a small tract society in Glasgow to a major Christian charity with an international influence is told in David Porter, *Go Deliver: The Blythswood Story* (Fearn, Ross-shire, 1992). The even more remarkable story of its principal founder, Rev. John

Liz does some administrative work in the seniors' health care field, but sees her primary role as that of a wife and mother of five children. James and Bett have been blessed with seven grandchildren and one great grandchild thus far.

James describes Bett as "absolutely extraordinary," recalling that she was a nurse and "when we got married she was willing to come and look after my father even although it meant she could not finish her course at the Royal Infirmary. She did [this] for six months or so before he passed away. I am very blessed and I try to be thankful for that. Our relationship has always been very happy and our family is very important to us. They have been supportive of us in every situation. For this I am very thankful."[6]

The Mackay home in Edinburgh was a place of generous hospitality to, among others, university students, including myself and other family members. I remember asking James how he took notes at university. His answer: "I didn't. I remembered the spoken word!" Another memory is of a question he asked those of us present, and then answered himself: "Why is it that the majority of the Ten Commandments are phrased negatively?" The answer, as

W. (Jackie) Ross, is told in Irene Howat, *An Irregular Candidate: Jackie Ross of Blythswood* (Fearn, Ross-shire: Christian Focus, 2002). Of the latter, Lord Mackay writes that it is "a fascinating account of a life in the Highlands of Scotland devoted to the care of soul and body of a huge variety of people... it is a frank insight into what made Jackie tick - a deep love for Christ and a warm wish that all he meets should know that love." Jackie Ross passed away from cancer in 2002.

6 "Lord Mackay of Clashfern Part 2: From Court Room to Cabinet Room." Interview with Robert Pirrie in *Signet Magazine: The Magazine of the Writers to Her Majesty's Signet*, February, 2013-Issue 4:19.

I recall, had something to do with the negative including or implying the positive. He also planted firmly in my mind the distinction between jealousy and envy, such that God is jealous (requiring exclusive possession and loyalty) of his people without being envious of other "gods." A less happy memory is of my leaning back on an antique dining room chair and breaking it!

Lord Advocate of Scotland

One Friday in 1979, James and Bett Mackay were shopping at Marks and Spencer (a British chain store), when they ran into a professional colleague who said, "James, I hear you're going to be Lord Advocate." James responded with an astonished "What!" and said he rather wished he had been informed. Sure enough, the following Monday he received a phone call from Prime Minister Margaret Thatcher, inviting

A current rear view of the former Mackay home in Edinburgh
Courtesy of present owners and the Saville website
www.rightmove.co.uk

him to take on the position of Lord Advocate, the chief legal officer of the government and crown in Scotland. He accepted and took the title of Lord Mackay of Clashfern in honour of his father's first home.

Normally, the governing party in parliament would choose one of its own party members for the position, but James Mackay was not known for his political affiliation. The obvious choice, based on precedent, would have been Nicholas Fairbairn, Q.C., who was a Conservative Member of Parliament. Mackay suggested this to the Prime Minister and she replied that if he (Mackay) would take on the top job, Fairbairn could be appointed to the deputy position of Solicitor General.

Fairbairn was a flamboyant and controversial political figure, such that the Prime Minister did not feel she could safely rely on him to be in charge of the senior office. This led to his being passed over in favour of Mackay. It is significant that both Conservative Prime Minister Thatcher and her Labour predecessor James Callaghan (Prime Minister, 1976-79) were inclined to appoint Mackay. Fairbairn was no doubt disappointed at having been passed over, but he would later describe Mackay as possessing "extraordinary good manners" as well as being "incredibly intelligent."[7]

As Lord Advocate, Mackay was head of the Scottish

---

7   Sir Nicholas Fairbairn in BBC program, "Make Way for the Lord Chancellor 1," https://www.youtube.com/watch?v=lj9c5aB8MQU. Uploaded May 17, 2010.

prosecution service and also represented the United Kingdom in the European Court of Justice. He gained a considerable reputation in the English legal establishment, and is credited with creating English interest in many aspects of Scots law.

Reflecting in an interview with *Signet Magazine* on his time as Lord Advocate, Mackay had this to say:

> I think it was very good for me. I was introduced to the world of politics and to the matters of the press and so on and introduced to it fairly gently because I was fairly junior in the political hierarchy... I worked a lot with Sir Michael Havers [then Attorney General and later Lord Mackay's predecessor as Lord Chancellor] and he used to nominate me for doing English cases in the House of Lords and the Court of Justice of the European Community. That was an extraordinary experience and maintained my position as an Advocate quite a bit even after being the Lord Advocate.... So I continued to be an Advocate really until I became a judge in 1984.[8]

The appointment as judge was jointly to the Court of Session, the supreme civil court of Scotland and to the High Court of Judiciary, the supreme criminal court. This was followed in 1985 by an appointment as a Lord of Appeal in Ordinary ("Law Lord") of the House of Lords.

---

8   "Lord Mackay of Clashfern, Part 1: From the Highlands to High Office," July 2012-Issue 3:19.

The House of Lords (or House of Peers) is the upper house of the British parliament. Unlike the House of Commons where Members of Parliament are elected, representing local constituencies in the United Kingdom, the current lords are mostly appointed. Prior to the House of Lords Act of 1999, all hereditary peers were also entitled to sit in the Lords. The Labour government of the day tried to have them all removed, but compromised by allowing 92, elected among themselves, to remain until all proposed reforms would be complete. However, so far this has not happened.

The membership of the House of Lords is comprised of Lords Spiritual and Lords Temporal. Lords Spiritual are 26 bishops in the established Church of England. The majority of Lords Temporal are appointed by the monarch on the advice of the Prime Minister. A large part of their role is to scrutinise bills that have been approved by the House of Commons. Bills may also be introduced first in the Lords. All bills must be passed by both houses of parliament before being enacted into law by royal assent, except in exceptional cases where, by virtue of the Parliament Acts, the consent of the House of Lords is dispensed with. Members of the Lords may also serve as government ministers. Until 2009 and the establishment of the Supreme Court of the United Kingdom, twelve Law Lords served as the highest court of appeal in the United Kingdom. It was as one of these twelve that James Mackay was appointed.

There is a touching story associated with this appointment:

> I was sitting in Glasgow, in the High Court,
> a criminal trial, and I was coming home
> from court in the afternoon walking up
> [Argyle] Street. That morning's papers had
> my appointment and, as I recall, there was a
> big photograph in the Daily Record.... [T]wo
> chaps were sitting on a seat and as I passed
> one of them said, "Lord Mackay". So I came
> over to him and he said, "We see you got
> a wee bit of promotion — we were all very
> pleased". I didn't know for whom he was
> speaking! Anyway, I thanked him kindly then
> went on. There was something about [this]
> that really stirred my heart a bit.[9]

Lord High Chancellor

Next came the highest law office in the land, Lord High Chancellor of Great Britain.[10] James Mackay was sitting listening to a debate in the House of Lords when he received a message that the Prime Minister wished to see him as urgently as possible. He was asked to meet with her at 4.30 pm. Just after that time, he was met at the door of 10 Downing Street. Mrs. Thatcher was waiting upstairs. She said that Michael Havers had resigned as Lord Chancellor that afternoon on the grounds of ill health, having only

---

9   Ibid.
10   Great Britain consists of England, Wales and Scotland. Northern Ireland
     is part of the United Kingdom, but not of Great Britain. Although Lord
     Mackay was never the Lord Chancellor of Northern Ireland, his office had
     responsibility for the judiciary in Northern Ireland.

been appointed four months previously in May 1987, and "we want you" to become Lord Chancellor. He was thunderstruck, but said it was a great honour to be asked. He would like to ask his wife before giving a final answer. With Mrs. Thatcher sitting across from him, he lifted the telephone and gave the number to the operator at No. 10 and was put through to his Edinburgh home.[11] There was no answer.

Mrs. Thatcher asked to be informed as soon as he had spoken to Bett because, she said, "we would like to have the announcement on the 7 o'clock evening news." On returning to the House of Lords, Lord Mackay kept phoning at regular intervals. Eventually Bett answered (she had been shopping). He explained what was happening and they agreed that, as Bett put it, "I don't think you can refuse." James recalls, "I phoned the Private Secretary who insisted on putting the call through to the Prime Minister. I told her that I had spoken with Bett and that I would be delighted to take the appointment. Mrs. Thatcher thanked me and said the announcement would be on the 7 o'clock news... It was quite a day, I can tell you!"[12]

Two or three weeks later, the Mackays were invited to lunch with the Speaker of the House of Commons. On their way, they discovered that Mrs. Thatcher and her husband

---

11 James and Bett had by this time moved out of their family home into an apartment near the Palace of Holyroodhouse (the Queen's official residence in Edinburgh) and the Scottish parliament buildings.

12 "Lord Mackay of Clashfern Part 2: From Court Room to Cabinet Room," 15-17.

Lord and Lady Mackay during his tenure as Lord Chancellor

were to be at the lunch as well. When the Thatchers arrived, James introduced Bett as "the lady who kept us waiting." Mrs. Thatcher bowed very low and said to Bett, "We are very grateful for your answer."[13] Despite her willingness, Bett found it difficult moving to London and embracing her new role there, but she recognised it to be a privilege. She also developed new and enduring friendships with people around the world.

Among the many congratulations received on James's appointment was a telegram from a pool hall in Glasgow, reading "Good luck, sir, in your new job! You'll need it! From the Glasgow boys." As noted above, Lord Mackay treasured such sentiments from "real people." The esteem of his colleagues can be gauged from an inscription in his copy of the first *Denning Law Journal* published the previous year by Lord Denning, formerly Master of the Rolls

---

13   Ibid.

(i.e. President of the Court of Appeal). Denning wrote, "For James Mackay with high esteem in the sure confidence that he will long adorn the Lords and give the best of advice to all generations. And in much appreciation of his kindness and all best wishes. Tom Denning."

At his first press conference as Lord Chancellor, James Mackay made it clear that he saw his role as one of serving the judges. He spoke of the need for improved working conditions and lifted restrictions prohibiting judges from speaking to the press. He also addressed child-care law reform and the more controversial issue of prison reform. "If you are humane and compassionate at heart, and judges should be," he said, "it is an awesome responsibility to send [individuals] to prison knowing the conditions they will face when they arrive at the prison gate." He suggested the possibility of alternative forms of punishment for nonviolent offenders. In a separate action, the new Lord Chancellor announced measures to improve payments to lawyers involved in legal aid cases.[14] As Lord Chancellor, James Mackay was one of the most senior ministers in the British Cabinet, the speaker of the House of Lords, and most significantly, the person normally responsible for nominating judicial appointments in England, Wales and Northern Ireland. He was not the first Scot to be appointed Lord Chancellor, but he was the first who had previously

---

14   This paragraph is from an article I wrote, based on unnamed newspaper reports, in *WORLD*, January 18, 1988, reprinted as "MacKay (sic) Named Lord Chancellor" in the *CLS (Christian Legal Society) Quarterly*, Spring 1988: 26.

Margaret Thatcher (1925-2013) Prime Minister (1979-90)
Provided by Chris Collins of the Margaret Thatcher Foundation

practiced only at the Scottish Bar. Nicholas Fairbairn opined that if an Englishman had been appointed to a comparable position in Scotland, it would have led to a revolution![15] However, there was general recognition that Mackay was simply the best man for the job. Besides, as an outsider to the political hierarchy, he owed no one any favours. Margaret Thatcher considered him to be "the best lawyer in my government." The President of the Law Society of Scotland stated, "He is not only an outstanding man in his profession, but one of the most brilliant Scottish scholars of

15   Sir Nicholas Fairbairn in BBC program, "Make Way for the Lord Chancellor" 2, http://www.youtube.com/watch?v=jY8NmQzvv1o. Uploaded May 18, 2010.

all time."[16]

Several years later, following the death of Baroness Thatcher who after her resignation as Prime Minister would join Lord Mackay in the House of Lords, he and others paid tribute to her. As part of his tribute, he recalled an amusing incident:

> In those days, the position of Lord Chancellor to which I was appointed had a certain priority [in] protocol. Shortly after my appointment, my wife and I were invited to a state function at Buckingham Palace. At that time, the protocol was—it may still be, for all I know—that the first couple to greet the Queen and the royal guests from the other country was the Archbishop of Canterbury and his wife. The second couple to go in was the Lord Chancellor and his wife, and the Prime Minister followed. My wife could hardly contain herself at the idea of going in front of Margaret Thatcher into the royal presence. Mrs Thatcher just said to her, "This is what you have to do. On you go". My wife had to do what she was told. Her [Thatcher's] character did not allow for much debate on that kind of thing.[17]

Lord Mackay was to become the longest continuously serving Lord Chancellor of the twentieth century (1987-97),

---

16 These quotations are from my article, "MacKay (sic) Named Lord Chancellor."
17 House of Lords, 10 April 2013. "Death of a Member: Baroness Thatcher," Column 1161. Lords Hansard Text for 10 April 2013, www.parliament.uk.

having been reappointed in 1990 by Thatcher's successor, John Major, (the same year in which he became an honorary member of the American College of Trial Lawyers). An interesting detail in Major's autobiography is his mention of Lord Mackay's role in the decision to return the Stone of Scone, also known as the Stone of Destiny, to Scotland on St. Andrews Day 1996. Ancient kings of Scotland had been crowned on this stone. It was taken as booty by Edward I of England in 1296 and placed under the chair in Westminster Abbey where British sovereigns are crowned. On Christmas Day 1950, four Scottish students broke into the Abbey and stole the stone, returning it to Scotland and placing it eventually on the altar of Arbroath Abbey in the safekeeping of the Church of Scotland. When the police were informed of its whereabouts, the stone was returned to Westminster Abbey. In 1996, as a symbolic response to growing nationalism in Scotland, it was decided by Major's Conservative Government that it would be returned to Scotland and kept there when not used at coronations. In considering the pros and cons of returning the stone, John Major consulted Lord Mackay, who advised that the advantages outweighed the disadvantages.[18]

Subsequently, following a referendum in 1997, the Labour Government then in power passed the Scotland Act 1998, resulting in the devolution of some powers to a reconstituted Scottish Parliament for the first time since the

---

18 See John Major, *The Autobiography* (New York: Harper Collins, 1999), 426-27.

Act of Union in 1707, when the Kingdom of Scotland had merged with the Kingdom of England to form the Kingdom of Great Britain. Labour Prime Minister Tony Blair, who was himself born in Scotland, hoped that this would mute the calls for Scottish independence. In fact, the effect was the reverse, as in 2007 the Scottish Parliament came under the control of the Scottish National Party, which arranged for a (failed) referendum on Scottish independence on November 18, 2014. Following the 2016 referendum by which the majority of the United Kingdom, but not of Scotland (or Northern Ireland), voted to leave the European Union, there have been further calls for another referendum on Scottish independence, although these have been somewhat muted by the results of the June 2017 general election.

When Lord Mackay first took his place in the House of Lords as Lord High Chancellor of Great Britain, he stated that it was a great honour, not just for him, but also for Scotland. However, for him, loyalty to Scotland means maintaining its union with England and Wales as part of Great Britain and with Northern Ireland as part of the United Kingdom. When asked about his views on the 2014 referendum on Scottish independence, he said:

> The Union has led to remarkable intertwining of our nations and the act of separation of itself is likely to cause damage. Two of our children live in England and will have no vote in the referendum. This illustrates how the ties of kinship will be broken by the process,

but this will be instantly repaired if the vote negatives independence. If not, this will be a permanent rupture of close relationships that will be damaging and permanent and repeated in countless families across the United Kingdom. Second, there are very strong ties of trade which will be damaged. A high proportion of Scottish trade is with England. Our currency, our defence, our position internationally are all shared. For example, our seat on the Security Council of the United Nations is held by the United Kingdom as is our membership of the EU and NATO. Third, the resources of the United Kingdom are much greater than those of Scotland and therefore what would be the consequence for a separate Scotland of a disaster such as the threat of collapse of two major banks? Although England is much bigger than Scotland, the part played by Scots in the United Kingdom has been considerable. I believe firmly that united we are much stronger than we would be separately. There is synergy in the Union.[19]

Like the majority of his fellow-Scots, Lord Mackay also opposed "Brexit," the 2016 referendum referenced above. When in a decision, later upheld by the Supreme Court, the High Court ruled that the government could

---

19 Personal email correspondence, July 30, 2013. In saying this, Lord Mackay was expressing in terms of current "secular" issues what John Knox had wished for before it happened, for largely theological reasons. See Alistair McConnachie, "Scottish Origins of British Unionism: John Knox's Unity of Monarchy and Faith," http://www.aforceforgood.org.uk/history/knox, posted 15 July, 2015.

not trigger Article 50 (the official notification to leave the European Union) without a vote in parliament, Lord Mackay characteristically came to the defense of the judges who had come under media attack, noting that the freedom of the press "does not entitle the press to insult, in a vicious and vocal manner, judges who are carrying out their statutory responsibilities."[20]

On the other hand, in a televised interview with the European Leadership Forum, two years previously, Lord Mackay had reflected on the challenges resulting from treaty obligations to honour the findings of the European Court of Human Rights in Strasbourg, France. Within the United Kingdom, laws can only be changed by parliament and the judiciary must respect those laws. In the context of the European Convention on Human Rights however, if a finding of the British judiciary is referred to Strasbourg for a ruling, the British parliament is obligated to consider adjusting its laws if necessary to accommodate that ruling. This, Lord Mackay mused, can lead to considerable difficulties for parliamentarians.[21]

During his tenure as Lord Chancellor, Mackay

---

20 https://www.theyworkforyou.com/lords/?id=2016-11-07a.928.1&s=speak er%3A13122#g935.0.

21 "An Interview with Lord Mackay - His Life and Career as a Politician," FOCL online, https://www.youtube.com/watch?v=na3qtD1sCWs, published on June 6, 2014. Lord Mackay later clarified that the British parliament must consider, but not necessarily to implement the judgements of the European Court of Human Rights. However, the decisions of the European Court of Justice are binding in British law, as long as the United Kingdom remains in the European Union. Personal email, April 20, 2017.

The Lords debate the Brexit Bill
Credit: AFP/Getty Images. Published in The Telegraph, 7 March, 2017

introduced changes to the legal system of England and Wales that won him praise as a reformer responsible for the most radical reforms in 700 years, but also criticism for "dressing up minor tinkering as major reform" and of thereby "hindering much-needed change in the legal system."[22] He was perceived by some as "obsessed" with cost-cutting above all else. Barristers, whose previous monopoly on the right to conduct litigation in the higher courts was broken, permitting qualified solicitors to do so, appear to have felt especially threatened. (Traditionally, barristers in England and Wales, and advocates in Scotland, have had a distinctly

---

22 The quotations are from an article by Fiona Bawdon in *The Independent* newspaper, "Law: Do We Really Need a Lord Chancellor?" Friday 17 July 1994. See Ruth Fleet Thurman, "English Legal System Shake-Up: Genuine Reform or Teapot Tempest?" (*Boston College International and Comparative Law Review*, Vol. XVI No, 1), for a helpful discussion of the major changes made in 1990 and their "ripple effect as far away as the United States."

separate role from solicitors.)

The office of Lord Chancellor was unique in British politics. It straddled the executive, legislature, and judiciary. The incumbent was a judge, cabinet minister and parliamentarian. Lord Mackay saw this as being crucial to the preservation of judicial independence. It meant that he was "able to act both as a bridge and as a fortification between the executive and the judicial powers."[23] However, there was increasing criticism by those who saw the office as either too powerful or anachronistic. This led ultimately to its being reduced to only a cabinet ministry by the New Labour government of Tony Blair, as part of its broader reforms of the House of Lords. A Secretary of State for Constitutional Affairs was appointed alongside. According to one of Blair's biographers, not only was the judiciary offended by this development with the "loss of its 'champion' in Cabinet," the Queen was also reported to be "hopping" about it![24]

In ancient times the office of Lord Chancellor had been held by clerics, including Sir Thomas More (1478-1535). In the sixteenth century, the Dutch Renaissance humanist Disederius Erasmus said of Lord Chancellor

---

23 Quoted by Fiona Bawdon, Ibid. See also Lord Mackay's remarks in his lecture on "The Judges" in The Administration of Justice published under the auspices of The Hamlyn Trust. London: Stevens & Sons/Sweet & Maxwell, 1994, 18: "The fact that the executive and judiciary meet in the person of the Lord Chancellor should symbolise what I believe is necessary for the administration of justice in a country like ours, namely a realisation that both the judiciary and the executive are parts of the total government of the country with functions which are distinct but which must work together in a proper relationship if the country is to be properly governed."
24 Anthony Seldon, Blair Unbound (London: Simon & Schuster, 2007), 218.

William Warham (c.1450-1532), who was also Thomas Cranmer's predecessor as Archbishop of Canterbury, "As often as he goes into public, a crown and sceptre are carried before him. He is the eye, the mouth-piece and the right hand of the Sovereign, and the supreme judge of the whole British empire."[25] By Lord Mackay's time, and for some considerable time before, the office was held by lawyers, but there was still a connection with the established Church of England, in that one of the Lord Chancellor's duties was the nomination of priests to local parishes, as well as to some other ecclesiastical positions. The actual details were dealt with by the ecclesiastical secretary to the Prime Minister, but Lord Mackay had the responsibility of establishing the policy which, no doubt reflecting his Presbyterian background, was that the people should choose the priest, and "it's amazing how well that worked!"[26]

Church Conflict

It was during his tenure as Lord Chancellor that James Mackay faced one of the most difficult and painful episodes in his life. As indicated earlier, he had grown up in the Free Presbyterian Church of Scotland. He would in time serve that denomination as an elder in the Edinburgh congregation and as a legal adviser and assistant clerk of Synod, where he served alongside his long-time friend Rev. R.R. Sinclair, the distinguished Synod clerk and a

---

25   Quoted in Alastair Bruce, *Keepers of the Kingdom: The Ancient Offices of Britain* (London: Weidenfield and Nicolson 1999), 42.
26   See above, "An Interview with Lord Mackay – His Life and Career as a Politician."

beloved senior minister, with whom James Mackay was to maintain weekly telephone calls throughout his career. Mackay saw his role at Synod as that of a peacemaker, often offering mediating positions on controversial issues. I recall witnessing one debate during which Sinclair and another close friend of Mackay expressed strongly opposing views, Sinclair in particular rising to heights of impassioned oratory in opposing what he saw as an unbiblical sectarianism. In his typically calm manner, late in a heated debate, Mackay sorted out the merits of both positions, "on the one hand... on the other hand."

The Free Presbyterian Church is often confused with the "wee frees," which was the moniker given to those members of the Free Church who did not merge with the United Presbyterian Church in 1900 to form the United Free Church. The Free Presbyterians had already left the Free Church in 1893 over a watering down of that denomination's adherence to the *Westminster Confession of Faith*. The "wee frees" shared the same concerns, but waited until the 1900 merger took place before withdrawing from the majority. The Free Presbyterian Church of Scotland also should not be confused with the denomination of the same name founded by the late Rev. Iain Paisley in Northern Ireland.

The late F.F. Bruce, in reviewing histories of the Free Church and the Free Presbyterian Church, noted that "the Free Presbyterian Church showed itself well in advance of the current climate of opinion when, in 1963, it unanimously elected the Rev. Petros Mzamo... to be Moderator of Synod — the first occasion on which an African presided over the supreme court of any Church in Scotland, or possibly in the whole United Kingdom." Bruce professed "the highest regard for both Churches," observing that neither "enjoys a good press; but they may console themselves that they are unlikely to incur the woe pronounced by our Saviour on his disciples when all men speak well of them."[27]

James Mackay was a loyal Free Presbyterian. On one occasion, during student days, I mentioned a visitor to the Edinburgh congregation who appreciated the preaching of our pastor, Rev. Donald Campbell, but who was otherwise quite critical of the church. I said that he often spoke to me about the faults of the Free Presbyterian Church. James looked at me and responded sharply, "What are they? I'm not aware of them!" Even when in later life his public duties led him into conflict with denominational leadership, he referred to the church's principles as "the most tender love that has ever been described."[28]

The conflict arose because of a small notice in the *Daily Telegraph* of a memorial service for Lord Russell of Killowen in June 1986. Lord Russell was a Roman Catholic and Requiem Mass was celebrated. Among former colleagues in attendance was the future Lord Chancellor. The Free Presbyterians had always taken a strong stand

---

27 F.F. Bruce, "Reviews and Notices," *Evangelical Quarterly*, Vol. 47, (1975): 245.
28 BBC program, "Make Way for the Lord Chancellor 1."

against Roman Catholicism and, particularly, the sacrifice of the Mass.

The *Catechism of the Catholic Church* states that in the Eucharist:

> the sacrifice Christ offered once for all on the cross remains ever present....The Eucharist is thus a sacrifice because it re-presents (makes present) the sacrifice of the cross.... The sacrifice of Christ and the sacrifice of the Eucharist are one single sacrifice: "The victim is one and the same: the same now offers through the ministry of priests, who then offered himself on the cross; only the manner of offering is different." "And since in this divine sacrifice which is celebrated in the Mass, the same Christ who offered himself once in a bloody manner on the altar of the cross is contained and offered in an unbloody manner... this sacrifice is truly propitiatory."[29]

The *Catechism* goes on to quote the Council of Trent (1545-63) to the effect that: "Because Christ our Redeemer said that it was truly his body that he was offering under the species of bread, it has always been the conviction of the Church of God, and this holy Council now declares again, that by the consecration of the bread and wine there takes place a change of the whole substance of the bread into the substance of the body of Christ our Lord and of the whole substance of the wine into the substance of his blood. This

---

29 *Catechism of the Catholic Church* (New York: Doubleday), 380-81, quoting Council of Trent (1562): DS 1743; cf. Heb 9:14, 27.

change the holy Catholic Church has fittingly and properly called transubstantiation."[30] Because of this change in substance (although not in appearance), the sacrament calls forth "adoration and worship."[31]

Since the Second Vatican Council (1962-65), there has been considerably more dialogue than previously between the Roman Catholic Church and some Protestant denominations, resulting in (among other things) a softening of the traditional Protestant understanding of the Mass. For instance, Synod 2006 of the Christian Reformed Church in North America, after years of study and consultation with representatives of the Roman Catholic priesthood, "directed that Q&A 80 remain in the CRC's text of the Heidelberg Catechism but that the last three paragraphs be placed in brackets to indicate that they do not accurately reflect the official teaching and practice of today's Roman Catholic Church and are no longer confessionally binding on members of the CRC."[32] The offending paragraphs include the statement that "the Mass is basically nothing but a denial of the one sacrifice and suffering of Jesus Christ and a condemnable idolatry."[33] This statement of the *Heidelberg Catechism* reflects the traditional Protestant understanding, and it is to this understanding that the Free Presbyterian

---

30 Ibid., 384-85; cf. Council of Trent (1551): DS 1642; cf. *Mt* 26:26ff; *Mk* 14:22ff.; *Luke* 22:19ff.; *1 Cor* 11:24ff.

31 Ibid., 334.

32 *Acts of Synod 2006* (Grand Rapids, MI: Christian Reformed Church in North America), 711.

33 *The Heidelberg Catechism*, Lord's Day 30, Q & A 80 (Grand Rapids, MI: Faith Alive Christian Resources, 2011), 98.

Church continues to hold (although the *Heidelberg Catechism* is not one of its confessional documents).

The Free Presbyterian Synod had routinely condemned political leaders who had attended Mass "ranging from King Edward VII to Winston Churchill to [the] present Prince of Wales."[34] Now one of their own was guilty of the same. Mackay countered that he was not countenancing the Mass, but simply showing respect to a deceased colleague and friend. He had taken a professional oath to "do right to all manner of persons," and this is what he had done. He repudiated the errors of Rome and made a distinction between "watching a Mass and going forward to receive the Host."[35] This was not good enough. When he refused to guarantee that he would not do the same again (and he in fact did), a protracted discipline case ensued that received widespread media attention at home and was also reported in the international press. Finally, by a vote of 33 to 27, the Synod upheld a lower court's (the Southern Presbytery's) suspension of the one-time legal adviser and assistant clerk. Rev. Petros Mzamo, the African minister from the church's Zimbabwe mission elected as moderator in 1963, was also present on this occasion and compared witnessing Mass to attending ancestor worship. Another African minister Rev. Aaron Ndebele presided over the vote on Lord Mackay and briefly left the chair to speak in favor of

---

34 Macleod, op. cit., 123. There is anecdotal evidence of other Free Presbyterians attending Requiem Mass at Roman Catholic funerals without censure, but they were not in the public eye.

35 Ibid., 125.

suspension, stating, "He is my friend, but can I allow him to go near fire?"[36]

Clearly not all Free Presbyterians were in favor of disciplining Lord Mackay. Among those who had spoken and voted against suspension was his loyal friend, now in his nineties, R.R. Sinclair, who told reporters after it was over, "I went through the Great War; I'm not afraid of those boys in there!"[37] Prior to the Synod's decision, a considerable internal debate had ensued, with pamphlets being published and a petition in Lord Mackay's favour receiving widespread circulation. In the end, several supporters of the Lord Chancellor separated from the denomination, charging it with having violated the teaching of its *Confession of Faith* on liberty of conscience. Lord Mackay himself made it clear that he had not encouraged the formation of the newly formed Associated Presbyterian Churches and, although he and his wife worship regularly in the Inverness congregation when they are at home, they have never formally joined.

Although exceedingly painful at the time, James and Bett now look back on this difficult period in their lives as providentially opening them up to the wider evangelical church. In London they often worshiped at All Souls Church of England, and formed a close friendship with its then rector the Rev. Dr. John R. W. Stott. James recalls with pleasure how on one occasion when he was a Scripture reader, Stott told him that they were sharing together in the ministry of

36 Ibid., 144.
37 Ibid., 145.

the Word. It was during this time that James was introduced to evangelist Billy Graham. He subsequently chaired a Luis Palau crusade. These are things he would never have done, or been permitted to do, as a Free Presbyterian. James now says of the whole experience that when one is in a building one only sees the light within, but when one leaves the building one is exposed to the brightness of the light outside. This should not be interpreted as a compromising of basic principles, but as a greater appreciation of what the *Westminster Confession of Faith* calls the "fellowship of the saints."

John R.W. Stott, CBE (1921-2011)
Photo owned by Langham Partnership International

Because of the negative publicity his discipline case resulted in for his former denomination, Lord Mackay was reluctant to have it mentioned here and insisted that nothing critical should be said of his former colleagues. It was and is, however, very much part of his Christian experience, demonstrating his Christian character throughout.

Resignation and Continuing Influence

Following the calling of the general election in 1997, Lord Mackay resigned his position. He and his wife moved to the picturesque Highland community of Cromarty and then to the Highland capital of Inverness, where they presently live. He is Patron of the University of the Highlands and Islands Development Fund. In 1991 he had been appointed as Chancellor of Heriot-Watt University in Edinburgh and held that position for fourteen years. (In the British university system, the office of chancellor is a ceremonial non-resident position.) His last official act as Chancellor, on the instruction of the Senate of the University, was to confer an honorary degree on his wife in recognition of her contribution to the university during his tenure.[38]

As noted previously, Lord Mackay has continued to be active in the House of Lords, frequently flying south to participate in debates. He also served for a number of years as editor of *Halsbury's Laws of England,* a regularly updated authoritative encyclopaedia of the laws of England and Wales. He was installed a Knight of the Thistle in 1999 at a ceremony presided over by the Queen at St. Giles Cathedral in Edinburgh. Previously, in 1984, he had been elected a Fellow of the Royal Society in Edinburgh, and in 2003 received its Royal Medal. Then, in 2007, Lord Mackay was

38 For the years of Lord Mackay's own honorary degrees, as well as other honours, see Foreword.

appointed as Lord Clerk Register and Keeper of the Signet, now a largely honourific office in Scotland with origins in the 13th century.

In 2005 and 2006, he served as Lord High Commissioner (the Queen's representative) to the General Assembly of the Church of Scotland. He is a past president and the patron of the Lawyers' Christian Fellowship based in London, and is currently Honorary President of the Scottish Bible Society. As part of its 2011 celebration of the 400th anniversary of the King James Bible, the society distributed copies of the (NIV) Bible to various courts and legal offices in Scotland. The Bibles were accompanied by a pamphlet, *The Bible in Scots Law: A Guide for Legal Practitioners*, with a foreword by Lord Mackay stating that: "I believe the teaching of the Bible is vitally important for guidance in daily living for all of us.... I have found it immensely important in my life and I trust it will be the same with many who have access to it through this initiative now."[39]

Not surprisingly, the initiative and Lord Mackay in particular, were subjected to considerable criticism and scorn, with critics labelling the campaign "an attempt to drag the legal system back to the 'dark ages'" and likening it to "a plea for a fundamentalist Christian version of Middle Eastern Sharia law."[40] But it is Lord Mackay's belief that if we use the Bible in dealing with our day-to-day challenges,

39 Foreword to *The Bible in Scots Law: A Guide for Legal Practitioners*. Scottish Bible Society, Edinburgh, www.scottishbiblesociety.org.
40 Mark Horne, "Law chief urges Scots courts: consult the Bible in judgments," *Sunday Herald*, 15 August, 2010.

"we will soon learn that what it says about human beings is as true today as it was when it was originally written all these years ago." This remains his abiding conviction and the controlling principle of his life.

3
Learning from Lord Mackay

WHEN JAMES MACKAY WAS APPOINTED LORD ADVOCATE of Scotland in 1979, Margaret and I paid a visit to the Mackay home in Edinburgh, where I conducted an interview for a forthcoming magazine article. James then drove us

Photo: James Campbell

to Waverley train station to board a train for Glasgow as the next step on our return to Canada. We were running late and James was helping us get our suitcases on the train as it was about to leave, urging us to "hurry, please!" Margaret turned and asked if he had any parting advice for us. In answer, he quoted Proverbs 3:6, "In all thy ways acknowledge him, and he shall direct thy paths."

Christian Character

The verse immediately preceding the one quoted above makes it clear that we are not to lean on our own understanding, but to trust in the Lord with all our hearts. This is what James Mackay has sought to do all of his professional life. Another Scripture that has served as a life verse is James 1: 5, "If any of you lack wisdom, let him ask of God, that giveth to all men liberally, and upbraideth not; and it shall be given him." Consistent with this, Lord Mackay has become known in the legal profession, in political circles and in the media as well as in the church, for his unassuming humility, personal loyalty, and gracious character.

An incident recorded by my brother-in-law John Tallach illustrates this point. Soon after he and my sister Isobel moved to a pastorate in Aberdeen in 1979, they had a visit from a man named Eric McCracken who represented a missionary organization. Before joining this organization, McCracken had worked as a court reporter in Edinburgh. He told John and Isobel about some of his experiences in his former life. He belonged to a team of shorthand writers who served in the courts. They would take down what was being said by lawyers and witnesses. They worked under considerable pressure, for short periods at a time, then were relieved so that they could go off and write up from their notes a record of the court's proceedings. McCraken said that it was not uncommon for lawyers to discuss with court reporters the terms in which the court's proceedings were to be reported. Some of them would treat the court reporters like dirt, ordering them to change what they had written to reflect what these lawyers wanted entered in the record. There was, however, one lawyer who always treated the reporters with respect. His name was James Mackay. He was probably the most able of all the lawyers, but if there was ever a question about what was to be entered in the court record he would come in and discuss the problem with the reporter as an equal and they would work towards a record with which they were both happy. "It was a recognised fact in the reporters' room," said McCracken, "that he had a humble attitude, and that he treated us with dignity."[1]

As Sir Nicholas Fairbairn noted, James Mackay was known among his colleagues to have "extraordinarily good manners." That this was recognised well beyond his professional colleagues is evidenced by the warm appreciation expressed to him by "real people" referenced earlier. On one occasion, a Glasgow scrap dealer, who had attended a trial over which Lord Mackay presided, wrote

---

1   Based on personal email correspondence, July 13, 2013.

to express appreciation for the manner in which he had sentenced one particular young man "as if you were his father."

This aspect of James Mackay's public reputation cannot be overemphasised. It is significant that before Jesus spoke to his disciples of their calling to be salt and light in society, he taught them in the Beatitudes what Christian character (and therefore its influence) looks like (Matthew 5: 1-16). This is a recurring theme throughout the New Testament. In several of the epistles, lists of Christian character can be found in contrast to patterns of sinful behaviour (e.g. Romans 12: 9-21; Galatians 5: 16-26; Ephesians 4: 17-32; Philippians 2: 1-18; Colossians 3:1-4:6; 1 Peter 3:8-17; plus the entire book of James).

All too often, those who have made public stands for Christian values in society have either done so in a manner inconsistent with their profession, or have been found to be inconsistent in their personal lives. Such a charge has not and cannot be made against James Mackay.

In the Beatitudes, the second last one is "Blessed are the peacemakers, for they shall be called the children of God" (Matthew 5:9). Lord Mackay's reputation has been as a peacemaker in both church and state. But what of the next Beatitude: "Blessed are they which are persecuted for righteousness' sake: for theirs is the kingdom of heaven..." (10-12)? Christians in the western world, living off the capital of its Christian heritage, are not persecuted to any extent like those suffering from the oppression of militant Islam, Communism, or other forms of anti-Christian hostility. There is, however, a growing harassment of Christians who take public stands against the spiritual and moral decline of our society. Lord Mackay has experienced some of that, as in his participation in the 400th anniversary celebration of the King James Bible. He is also no stranger to public criticism from church and state.

Jesus warned his disciples to beware when all people spoke well of them (Luke 6:26). But Scripture also teaches that when a man's ways please the Lord, he makes even his enemies to be at peace with him (Proverbs 16:7). Finding the biblical balance between these two principles can be particularly acute for those holding public office in a professedly secular state. They need to be sure that any persecution that comes their way is for Christ's sake and not any indiscretions on their part. Two other biblical principles that Lord Mackay has exemplified are to be wise as serpents and harmless as doves (Matthew 10:16), and to turn the other cheek when under attack (Matthew 9:39).

One characteristic of Lord Mackay's Christian profession that sets him apart from many other public Christians has been his consistent observance of the Lord's Day as a day of rest and worship. Perhaps in our modern society where business and politics as usual go on seven days a week, this is one of the most difficult areas of Christian witness for those in the public arena. However, newspaper reporters as well as colleagues soon learned that, in the words of Mackay's press agent when Lord Chancellor, "He's an extremely tolerant man, but he won't budge on that one."[2] Among other benefits of a weekly day of rest, Lord Mackay found it to be a good antidote to having too high an opinion of oneself.

Public Record

Prior to his appointment as Lord Advocate, James Mackay saw his role as that of a working lawyer representing various cases, bringing his legal and intellectual resources to bear on the issue at hand. Subsequently, and especially after his appointment as Lord Chancellor, he took on a more political role, representing the Conservative government and guiding its agenda through the House of Lords. Since resigning that position, he has continued to be an active member of the Lords, still representing the Conservative party, but not afraid to differ at times on matters of principle.

A thorough examination of all issues addressed by Lord Mackay both within and outside of government must await a more substantial review of his life and work. There is a vast amount of material to choose from, covering a wide range of human life, from its beginning (fertilisation and embryology) to its end (euthanasia and assisted suicide). In what follows, while far from comprehensive, I have chosen to focus on a few issues that evidence a common

---

2   Quoted in Cal McCrystal, "Profile: the Lord Chancellor is a tireless legal reformer, but only six days a week," *The Independent*, Sunday 12 December, 1993.

theme which seem to me to reflect the Christian character discussed above. We will first take note of a recurring concern for families in general and child welfare in particular. (This is a value shared by other Christians in public office, but not all who are politically conservative, as Lord Mackay is, demonstrate the same concern for the effects of poverty on families and single parents.) Then we will notice how Lord Mackay would often seek to find common ground on contentious moral issues when a principled compromise seemed to be the only realistic option.

Child Support: Our previous chapter began with a reference to Lord Mackay leading a "revolt" against the government of the day that he represented in the House of Lords. This was over changes to the Child Support Agency that would have the potential effect of forcing single parents to pay the government for collecting child support payments on their behalf. Writing in *The Telegraph* the day the vote took place in the Lords, Mackay stated that the step he was taking in proposing an amendment to the government legislation "was not taken lightly." But, he continued,

> I still remain convinced that the government's charging proposals are deeply unfair to parents raising children alone and will take away money intended for children.... I fully support constructive measures designed to assist former married and cohabiting partners, as well as parents who have never lived together, to collaborate better

for the good of their children where this is possible. My concern, however, is the plight of children where such collaboration fails or is impossible to achieve and where the other parent is unwilling to contribute properly to the children's upkeep.

Citing a briefing for peers in which the government acknowledged that "a significant proportion of parents will not be able to collaborate" in the new arrangement whereby separated parents would need to make their own arrangements to receive child support, Lord Mackay stated:

> It appears wrong to me in principle that children should be made to pay the price for the failure of the non-resident parent to accept his responsibilities. In my view, the State has a fundamental responsibility to step in to protect the interests of children and reinforce parental responsibility if necessary, without parents in need being charged for the privilege....
>
> My amendment would still allow charges: but would ensure that the burden falls where it deserves to be – on the parents whose failure to meet their responsibilities towards their children has made state intervention necessary.[3]

Family Law Bill: Concern for children of divorced and separated parents was also behind Lord Mackay's

---

3   "Comment: Lord Mackay criticises welfare reform plans," telegraph.co.uk. 25 Jan, 2012.

1995 Family Law Bill, which received considerable public criticism, especially from fellow-Christians who accused him of promoting no-fault divorce, contrary to Scripture. This bill aimed to remove allegations of fault as a basis for an often speedy divorce and instead made irretrievable breakdown of marriage the only ground, introducing a one-year waiting period during which information meetings would take place, advocating mediation.[4] The Anglican and Catholic bishops supported this effort, but evangelicals generally opposed it, as did some of Lord Mackay's fellow peers and cabinet ministers. His former denomination opined, "Despite the statements of good intentions from the Lord Chancellor, the Bill with its provision for no fault divorce, is a further and great departure from the scriptural standard. The Bible allows only two grounds for divorce, adultery and wilful desertion (Matthew 19:8-9; 1 Corinthians 7:15), but as the Westminster Confession of Faith (WCF) asserts, '... the corruption of man be such as is apt to study arguments, unduly to put asunder those whom God hath joined together in marriage... (WCF 24:6).'"[5] However, Lord Mackay was at pains to point out that his goal was the strengthening of marriage, not its dissolution. His personal preference was that there would be no divorce at all, but he believed

---

4   The existing law actually stipulated a two-year waiting period, but this was often not followed in practice. "The case for reform is that the law is mocked, since most couples divorce within months on often trumped-up and damaging accusations of unreasonable behaviour." Polly Tonybee, "Lord Mackay's well-intentioned fiasco," *The Independent,* Tuesday 24 October, 1995.

5   "Report of the Religion and Morals Committee," Rev. N. Ross, Convenor, *Free Presbyterian Church of Scotland, Reports of the Standing Committees, Submitted to Synod in May 1996,* 8.

that it would make divorce less acrimonious to insist on a longer waiting period and information meetings aimed at promoting mediation. He stated in a press conference, "I am deeply committed to life-long marriage as an ideal. However, I recognise that the civil law must accommodate many situations which, although less than ideal, do occur in practice. Marriage breakdown is such a situation, and the law must provide for an orderly and considered process of dissolution where that breakdown is irretrievable." He hoped that the removal of the incentive to allege fault — used for divorce in three-quarters of cases — would "remove the bitterness, hostility and sense of injustice which so often surrounds divorce."[6] Such an atmosphere "cannot help a couple consider whether divorce is the right course of action or indeed try to save their marriage. Even if the marriage has broken down irretrievably, how can such an atmosphere help the couple consider the consequences of divorce and make workable arrangements for the future for their children? I see no merit, either moral, intellectual or practical, in retention of the requirement to make allegations of fault in order to establish breakdown and do so quickly." Citing our Lord's allusion to Mosaic legislation on divorce, Lord Mackay opined that "our Lord's teaching contemplated a civil system in which it would be possible to do what He told His questioners should not be done."[7]

In a personal email in later years, he wrote, "I was

---

6   Stephen Ward, "Welcome for Mackay divorce reforms," *The Independent*, Thursday 27 April, 1995.

7   See Appendix 1.

dealing with the civil law and what was suited to our time. In practice by 1995 allegations of fault were never tried by the Court and they could have the effect of further damaging relations between the spouses, which was damaging to children of the marriage. I had provided that suitable arrangements had to be made for the children before the divorce was granted, which generally had to be a year before the divorce was granted. The bill passed into law with a large majority. It was not liked by those who wished quick easy divorce and was ultimately repealed."[8]

To be fair, it was not only those who "wished quick easy divorce" who opposed the bill. Several critics argued that it would lead to "divorce on demand" which Lord Mackay denied, but subsequent developments appear to have proved the critics correct. Lord Mackay's successor revoked the law and a spokesman from his office observed perceptively, "The reduction of acrimony and the adoption of a more conciliatory approach to divorce may require a cultural change beyond the realms of legislation."[9] However, it cannot be seriously doubted that Lord Mackay's goal was not to make divorce easier, but to provide for mediation and in particular to protect children damaged by acrimonious divorce proceedings. If this were not so, he would hardly have been supported by the Catholic bishops who, after he addressed them, issued a press release noting, "The Catholic

8   Personal email, August 22, 2016.
9   Quoted in "Government abandons law allowing 'no fault divorce'" by Robert Verkaik, Legal Affairs Correspondent, *The Independent*, 17 January, 2001.

Media Office has written to all the Catholic members of Parliament pointing out that the Lord Chancellor's White Paper on divorce law reform was broadly welcomed by the Catholic Bishops Conference."[10] Even a highly critical newspaper article recognised that Lord Mackay was "an honourable man... so utterly ingenuous by nature."[11]

A section of the Family Law Bill concerned domestic violence. It involved a revision of the 1994 Domestic Violence Family Homes Bill that had been dropped by the government. This bill had been opposed by some on what Lord Mackay believed to be the mistaken belief "that cohabitants were being placed on an equal footing with married couples for the first time, and that this undermined the institution of marriage." Although he did not think that the bill would have had the effect feared, Lord Mackay accepted that there was genuine concern to uphold the special nature of marriage. He shared this concern and for that reason made four changes to the previous bill. His speech in the House of Lords at the second reading of the Family Law Bill is printed as an appendix to this book, so that readers can see its intentions for themselves.

Children and Same Sex Marriage: A further more recent example of Lord Mackay's concern for the welfare of children is found in the debate on a Same Sex (Marriage) Bill, which ultimately became law in July 2013. Lord Mackay was an outspoken critic of the bill as it moved through

---

10   Quoted in Tonybee, op. cit.
11   Ibid.

the House of Lords. Yet, recognizing that it would most likely pass, he proposed a number of amendments, one of which was to recognise a distinction between marriages by referring in the bill to "marriage (same sex couples)" and "marriage (opposite sex couples)." He insisted that this amendment was the very minimum necessary to recognise the "distinction that exists in fact between marriage for same sex couples and marriage for opposite sex couples." To think otherwise, he said, was to engage in fantasy.

Speaking at length of the effects on children, Lord Mackay offered as his opinion that opposite sex marriage was a "uniquely well designed system" for the birth, nurture and protection of children, and that "so far the state has not been able to devise a system which is equally effective."[12]

Personal Allowance: As recently as November 2016, Lord Mackay offered advice to the Conservative government on its administration of the personal allowance, which is the non-taxable amount of one's income. In an article titled "To help poorer people, the Chancellor should raise the marriage allowance, not the personal allowance," he observed:

> In my view, it is difficult to see how a Government which very properly wants to 'make Britain a country that works for

---

12   BBC TV live coverage of the House of Lords Debate, 8 July 2013. The amendment was termed a "wrecking amendment" (Lord Deben) that would deal a "fatal blow" to the bill's intentions, and would create "two classes of marriage" (Lord Alli). It was defeated by a vote of 314 to 119, and Lord Mackay accordingly withdrew further amendments that were conditional on the passage of the first one.

Photo courtesy of Robert Pirrie in "From the Highlands to High Office,"
Signet Magazine: The Magazine of the Writers to Her Majesty's Signet,
The WS Society, Edinburgh, Part 1 July 2012. Issues 3.

everyone,' and which has particular regard for 'ordinary working class families', can take an additional £6 billion of public funds and then allocate approaching £4 billion of that sum to those in the top half of the income distribution, but only £2 billion to those in the lower half.

The principal reason why we have got into these distributional difficulties is that we are trying to help people on the basis of

individualistic personal allowances, which
have no regard for whether the person
concerned is single with no dependents,
or whether they have a family to support.
Income alone is no guide to where you stand
on the income distribution, because that
depends also on the number of mouths you
have to feed.

A far more progressive and targeted
approach to making Britain 'a country that
works for everyone' would be to invest in
a tax allowance that is cognisant of family
responsibility....

... If the Government feels bound to increase
the personal allowance to £12,500 then
it should at the very least rule that further
increases will be confined to taxpayers with
dependent children.[13]

Once again, Lord Mackay demonstrates his willingness to
differ with the priorities of the political party he continues
to represent in the House of Lord.

Amendments on Same-Sex Marriage: Besides his
concern for families and children, another characteristic
of Lord Mackay that the examples of divorce and same-sex
marriage in particular illustrate has been a desire to find
common ground in areas of legal ethics where a principled

---

13 http://www.conservativehome.com/platform/2016/11/james-mackay-
raising-the-marriage-allowance-helps-poorer-people-more-than-raising-
the-personal-allowance-which-is-why-the-chancellor-should-announce-it-
tomorrow.htm. Published: November 22, 2016.

compromise seemed to be the only realistic option available. Besides the amendment concerning the definition of marriage, another one would have exempted people from having to provide goods or services on occasions where doing so was in conflict with their conscience. He said: "Over the many years during which I have been involved in the law and the political process, people have often grumbled to me about aspects of our legal system. Until very recently I have always responded that in Britain, while there are matters about which people could be legitimately anxious, one could always be assured that the law would not require you to violate your conscience. In recent years, however, and certainly since 2006, this has been brought into question."

Giving the example of a Christian printer, Lord Mackay said that current equality legislation and the new bill put them in a "very difficult position" if they were approached by a gay rights organisation that was asking them to print material promoting same-sex sexual relations. He said that a gay printer would find himself in a similar position if approached by a Christian theologian who wanted him to print material calling same-sex sexual practice a sin. He pointed to the example of doctors who are allowed to refuse to perform abortions because of conscientious objections. "It is possible to have lots of things that are not genuine, but I am talking of a genuine conscientious objection which should be allowed."[14] Not surprisingly, Lord

14   Lord Mackay of Clashfern, Equality Bill – Committee (Continued) (2nd Day),

Mackay voted against proposed amendments that would have "watered down" existing provisions that allowed religious groups to "restrict jobs to believers and refuse to hire people whose private conduct is inconsistent with their teaching." The key amendments to change the law were defeated by the Lords in a vote of 216 to 178.[15]

Dr. C. Everett Koop (1916-2013)
US Surgeon General (1982-89)

Comparison with Koop: On the subject of principled compromise, especially as that relates to the controversy over divorce legislation, a somewhat comparable situation in American politics was the furore that erupted when the late Surgeon General, Dr. C. Everett Koop (1916-2013, Surgeon General, 1982-89)[16] advocated sex education and

---

13th January, 2010. https://www.theyworkforyou.com/lords/?id=2010-01-13a.574.0&s=speaker%3A13122#g591.0.

15 Christopher Hope, "Equalities Bill: Church leaders defeat Government over gay staff," (Whitehall Editor, *The Telegraph*, 26 Jan, 2010).

16 Koop's personality was much more direct and assertive than Mackay's, but on matters of principle and practice, the comparison still holds.

condom use as a means of preventing the spread of AIDS. Koop came to national attention through his partnership with Francis Schaeffer in the production of the book and film series *Whatever Happened to the Human Race?* He was by that time already well respected as a surgeon for ground-breaking surgery in separating Siamese twins. His strong opposition to abortion and advocacy on behalf of the disabled was well known in Christian circles. Evangelical Christians were thus delighted when President Reagan nominated him as Surgeon General in 1981. His nomination process followed a typical path with political conservatives supporting it and liberals strongly opposing it.

However, when, as one of his responsibilities, Koop took on the task of dealing with the new and growing AIDS epidemic, advocating condom use for homosexuals and other promiscuous singles "foolish enough" to not practice abstinence, the tables turned. Liberals like Senator Ted Kennedy who had opposed his nomination became staunch supporters, while some former friends abandoned him. In his autobiography, Koop recalls:

> Castigation by the *political* right, although disappointing and unpleasant, did not duly upset me; after all castigation seemed to be their business. But I did feel a profound sense of betrayal by those on the *religious* right who took me to task…. Everyone, or at least those who did not know me, said that I had changed. Conservatives said I had

changed and they were angry. Liberals said I had changed, and they were pleased. But I had not changed at all…. My whole career had been dedicated to prolonging lives, especially the lives of people who were weak and powerless, the disenfranchised who needed an advocate: newborns undoubtedly who needed surgery, handicapped children, unborn children, people with AIDS.[17]

Some Christian ethicists teach that one should never have to choose between greater and lesser evils. But, to quote J. I Packer, "Whatever may be true in the field of ethics, compromise in politics means not the abandonment of principle, but realistic readiness to settle for what one thinks to be less than ideal when it is all that one can get at the moment."[18] This was true of both Mackay and Koop in their respective roles.

Faith and Politics

Christians in public life in Britain tend to be less outspoken about their faith commitments than their American counterparts. I once asked Lord Mackay about this, and he said it might be construed as inappropriate to use one's position to publicise one's faith. By extension, he would have thought it inappropriate as Lord Chancellor to use his considerable power and influence to appoint judges based on religious or political considerations, as is often done in

---

17 C. Everett Koop, M.D., KOOP: *The Memoirs of America's Family Doctor* (New York: Random House), 216.

18 J. I. Packer, "How to Recognize a Christian Citizen," *The Christian As Citizen* (Christianity Today Institute, April 19, 1985), 7.

the highly politicised Supreme Court nomination process in the United States. Commenting on that process once during a panel discussion with the then Chief Justices of Canada and the United States, he observed that in America judges are selected based on their opinions, whereas in the United Kingdom they are selected based on their ability to form an opinion once they have heard all the evidence. He recalls that American Chief Justice Rehnquist quite liked that!

In 1994, Lord Mackay delivered the annual Hamlyn Trust series of four lectures on "The Administration of Justice," subsequently published in book form. In the first lecture, he further developed this thought, noting:

> The judicial role in our system is to determine cases according to the evidence and argument put in relation to the case, not according to predispositions or previously held opinions which the judges might have. Obviously every judge comes to a case with previous experience and opinions formed in the light of that experience. But the criterion for a good judge is, to my mind, the extent to which he is able to apply his judgment afresh to issues put before him and to relegate to the background any such pre-formed views. The tendency of prior examination, as one has observed in the United States, is to discover and analyse the previous opinions of the individual in detail. I question whether the standing of the judiciary in our country, or the public's confidence in it, would be

enhanced by such an enquiry, or whether any wider public interest would be served by it.

In discharging the responsibility of making or recommending judicial appointments, it is of the greatest importance that political views and affiliations are left out of account. I can say for myself, and I hope it is generally recognised to be a feature of appointments to the judiciary by the Prime Minister or the Lord Chancellor, that considerations of that kind do not enter into the appointment of judges in this country…. Our judiciary comprise a broad range of independent and fair-minded people with a considerable variety of attitudes and opinions.[19]

Some might consider it unrealistic to suggest that a judge's "attitudes and opinions" would not influence his or her verdicts, but the highly politicised system that exists in the United States has led to charges of judges legislating from the bench rather than interpreting existing law.[20] At the

---

19 The Rt. Hon. The Lord Mackay of Clashfern, *The Administration of Justice* (London: Stevens & Sons/Sweet & Maxwell. Published Under the Auspices of The Hamlyn Trust, 1994), 8-9.

20 In the United States, the President nominates judges to the Supreme Court (among others) and the Senate votes on them after an extensive vetting process. Most nominees are eventually approved, but there have been some notable exceptions over the years. One was Robert Bork, nominated by Republican President Ronald Reagan in 1987. Bork was rejected by a Democratically controlled Senate, after an extensive media campaign, such that the verb "bork" has entered into the vocabulary of American English, defined (to use one of the milder definitions) as to "attack (a candidate or public figure) systematically, especially in the media." More recently, following the unexpected death of conservative jurist Anton Scalia in early 2016, Democratic President Barak Obama nominated Merrick Garland, widely considered to be a judicial centrist. The Republican controlled

very least, by upholding the independence of the judiciary, Lord Mackay attempted to uphold the integrity of the office, and by not using his considerable powers of appointment (which an American president could only dream of), for political or ideological ends, he demonstrated his own personal integrity.

British Christians in political life generally approach their calling with less of a thought-out Christian philosophy of politics than, for instance, those who have been influenced by the Dutch theologian-politician Abraham Kuyper who served as Prime Minister of the Netherlands between 1901 and 1905. Kuyper developed an elaborate sociology of "sphere sovereignty" whereby each sphere of life—ecclesiastical, political, economic etc.—is independent and sovereign in its own sphere of influence, with all spheres being subject to the ultimate sovereignty of God. As he famously declared, "There is not a square inch in the whole domain of our human existence over which Christ, who is Sovereign over all, does not cry, Mine!"[21] To

Senate, however, refused to even have hearings prior to the presidential election in November. Subsequently, Republican President Donald Trump nominated Neil Gorsuch, who is more in the Scalia mold. Although Gorsuch was clearly qualified, the Democratic minority in the Senate, threatened to filibuster the upcoming vote, forcing the Republicans to change the rules so their nominee could be confirmed by a simple majority on April 7, 2017. This, despite the fact that Gorsuch had previously won unanimous support from Democrats and Republicans alike when nominated by Republican President George W. Bush to the United States Court of Appeals for the Tenth Circuit.

21 James D. Bratt, ed., *Abraham Kuyper: A Centennial Reader* (Grand Rapids, MI: Eerdmans, 1998), 488. Kuyper's influence has extended far beyond Dutch Reformed circles. One of his best known and most influential disciples was the late Charles Colson, one time "hatchet man" of US President Richard Nixon, turned Christian political crusader and prison

approach political life without a comparably developed Christian philosophy can lead to compartmentalising, where faith and politics have little to do with one another. This charge, however, cannot be made against Lord Mackay. One might differ with him, even strongly so, on certain issues, but it cannot be questioned that he has approached his professional as well as private life with a whole-hearted commitment to be formed by the teaching of Scripture in humble submission to his Lord.

Views on Church Establishment

James Mackay stands in the theological tradition of the *Westminster Confession of Faith*, and its chapter on "The Civil Magistrate." This was produced at a time of Puritan ascendancy and clearly presupposed a Christian society and government. The situation in Britain today is much different, as can be seen from the hostile reaction noted previously to the simple act of distributing Bibles to Scottish courts and law offices. How, then, is a Christian in public office to conduct himself in such a context?

Lord Mackay reflects on this in an article titled "Does Establishment Have a Future?"[22] After referencing our Lord's Great Commission (Matthew 28:18-20) as the basis for the church's presence among the nations, he discusses the development of and changes to the established Church

---

reformer. His bestselling *How Now Should We Live* (Wheaton, Ill: Tyndale House Publishers, 2004) was heavily influenced by Kuyper.

22 Lord Mackay, "Does Establishment have a Future," *Theos: Clear thinking on religion and society,* http://www.theosthinktank.co.uk/ comment/2013/05/13/does-establishment-have-a-future.

of England, where the reigning monarch is its Supreme Governor. He then asks, "What are the challenges this relationship faces today?" Noting the rise of secularism since the 1960s, he quotes the late Bishop Newbigin to the effect that "no state can be completely secular in the sense that those who exercise power have no beliefs about what is true and no commitment to what they believe to be right." He goes on to note, "True tolerance does not imply indifference to the truth. In a society which has been nourished in its deepest roots by the Christian faith and tradition, can it really be impossible to envisage, with Newbigin, 'a state that acknowledges the Christian faith as true, but deliberately provides full security for those of other views'?" Mackay also quotes the present Queen as saying, "The concept of our established Church is occasionally misunderstood and, I believe, commonly under-appreciated. Its role is not to defend Anglicanism to the exclusion of other religions. Instead the Church has a duty to protect the free practice of all faiths in this country."

The article in its entirety is printed as Appendix 2 in this book, so I shall not summarize further at this point. I would, however, offer the suggestion that it discusses a view of establishment that is considerably diluted from the original wording of the *Westminster Confession of Faith,* which did not envisage a situation where those of all faiths and none would be granted the protection of the state. It may in fact be closer to the revised version adopted by the Presbyterian Church in the United States. Certainly, it is compatible with the revised version of the *Belgic Confession*, which teaches that it is the state's responsibility to:

> punish evil people and protect the good. And being called in this manner to contribute to the advancement of a society that is pleasing to God, the civil rulers have the task, subject to God's law, of removing every obstacle to the preaching of the gospel and to every aspect of divine worship. They should do this while completely refraining from every tendency toward exercising absolute authority, and while functioning in the sphere entrusted to them, with the means belonging to them. They should do it in order that the Word of God may have free course; the kingdom of Jesus Christ may make progress; and every anti-Christian power may be resisted.[23]

In other words, it is the task of the *church* to advance the kingdom of God by the preaching of the Word of God and

---

23   *The Belgic Confession*, Article 36 in *Ecumenical Creeds and Confessions* (Grand Rapids, MI: CRC Publications). The Belgic Confession was written in 1561 and originally the wording of Article 36 included the following: "And the government's task is not limited to caring for and watching over the public domain but extends also to upholding the sacred ministry, with a view to removing and destroying all idolatry and false worship of the Antichrist; to promoting the kingdom of Jesus Christ; and to furthering the preaching of the gospel everywhere; to the end that God may be honored and served by everyone, as he requires in his Word." In 1958, the Synod of the Christian Reformed Church in North America replaced these words with the ones quoted above. The Reformed Church in America, on the other hand, has retained the original wording, "choosing to recognize that the confession was written within a historical context which may not accurately describe the situation that pertains today."

the resistance of every anti-Christian power. It is the *state's* responsibility to preserve and maintain an orderly and peaceful society in which the church is free to go about its God-given task (see 1 Timothy 2: 2-4).

4
Locating Lord Mackay

THIS ESSAY BEGAN WITH A FAMOUS QUOTE about two kings and two kingdoms in Scotland. We then briefly developed the idea of the two kingdoms as articulated by Luther and, more specifically, Calvin. We saw how Calvin's view of church-state relations was reflected in the *Westminster Confession of Faith*, and how that document was modified in an American context with its non-establishment of religion, popularly (if somewhat inaccurately) known as the separation of church and state. From there we returned to Scotland and the life work of James Mackay, one-time Lord Advocate of Scotland and Lord High Chancellor of Great Britain. We briefly outlined his life's work and then suggested some lessons that might have relevance beyond the British Isles.

In recent years, there has been a revival of interest in "two kingdoms doctrine," especially in Reformed circles in America. Unlike the historic version, the contemporary one is sometimes based on the biblical-theological argument that God established a "common kingdom" for all people in his covenant with Noah (Genesis 9) and a "redemptive kingdom" for people of faith in his covenant with Abraham

(Genesis 12).[1] This viewpoint has been heavily criticised by representatives of another movement known as neo-Calvinism that draws its inspiration from Abraham Kuyper (and thus sometimes known as Kuyperianism.)[2] As best-selling author Timothy (Tim) Keller, the "most popular Reformed preacher and author in America today,"[3] rightly points out, "while this controversy involves a relatively small number of authors and readers, it is well worth our attention because the Reformed evangelical world, though numerically small, has an outsized impact on the broader evangelical community through its educational institutions and publications, and because it is a window into the kind of debates over culture now dividing conservative Christians within a variety of traditions and denominations throughout the world."[4]

Keller begins by describing the fundamentalist withdrawal from society in the early part of the twentieth century. With others, he labels this "pietistic," or concerned with personal piety and evangelism at the expense of cultural engagement.[5] A change began in the mid-twentieth

1   See e.g. David VanDrunen, *Living in God's Two Kingdoms* (Wheaton, Ill: Crossway, 2010).
2   Examples of neo-Calvinist criticisms include John Frame, *The Escondido Theology: A Reformed Response to Two Kingdom Theology* (Whitefield Media Productions, 2011) and Ryan McIlhenny, editor, *Kingdoms Apart: Engaging the Two Kingdoms Perspective* (Phillipsburg, NJ: P & R, 2012).
3   Kate Shellnutt, http://www.christianitytoday.com/gleanings/2017/march/princeton-rescinds-tim-keller-kuyper-prize-women-ordination.html?utm_source=ctweekly.
4   Timothy Keller, *Center Church* (Grand Rapids: Zondervan, 2012), 188.
5   Pietism was a 17th century movement in Lutheranism, promoting godly living and missions in addition to sound doctrine, but the term has come to be used in the pejorative way Keller defines it.

century through the influence of Carl F. H. Henry, Francis Schaeffer and others who, following Kuyper, popularized the idea of a Christian worldview affecting all of life.

> The original proponents of Kuyperian worldview engagement tended to be liberal in their politics—favoring European-style centralized economies and an expansive government with emphasis on justice and rights for minorities. However, another "wing" of Christian worldview proponents emerged in the 1970s and 1980s in the United States—the Religious Right....The Religious Right made heavy use of the concept of worldview, as well as the notion of "transforming culture" but connected these ideas directly to political action in support of conservative policies.[6]

Keller also notes the influence of Kuyper on the Christian Reconstruction or Theonomy movement that argues for the permanent relevance of the Mosaic law on society. But this is quite different from Kuyper's own vision.

Keller references H. Richard Niebuhr's classic *Christ and Culture*, with its five models: Christ against culture; Christ of culture; Christ above culture; Christ and culture in paradox; Christ transforming culture. Keller reduces these models to four: the transformationalist model; the relevance model; the counterculturalist model; the two kingdoms model. The second and third of these models

---

6   Keller, Ibid., 187.

need not concern us, not because they are unimportant, but because they do not relate directly to our subject. Keller notes strengths and weaknesses of all four models. Weaknesses of the transformationalist (Christ transforming culture) model are that:

- the concept of "worldview" is too cognitive;

- it is often marked by an underappreciation of the church;

- it tends to be "triumphalistic, self-righteous, and overconfident in its ability to both understand God's will for society and bring it about";

- it has often "put too much stock in politics as a way to change culture";

- it "often doesn't recognize the dangers of power."[7]

Weaknesses of the two kingdoms model are that:

- it gives more weight and credit to the function of common grace than the Bible does;

- "[m]uch of the social good that Two Kingdoms people attribute to natural revelation is really the fruit of the introduction of Christian teaching—of special revelation if you will—into world cultures";

- this model "implies or teaches that it is possible for human life to be conducted on a religiously neutral basis";

- it produces a form of "social quietism," meaning that (quoting Kevin DeYoung) this model shows an "unwillingness to boldly call Christians to work for positive change in their communities and believe that change is possible." (This has been blamed for such things as the Southern Presbyterian Church's

---

7   Ibid., 199-201.

tolerance of slavery in the nineteenth century and South African Christians' support of apartheid in the twentieth);

- finally, this model "contributes to too great a hierarchy between clergy and lay people."[8]

Tim Keller. *Photo: Frank Licorice*

Keller goes on to suggest that *"proponents of each model should do their best to discern and incorporate the insights of the other models."*[9] He believes that "each model has at its core a unique insight about the world and a fundamental truth from the Bible that any professing Christian must acknowledge. And therefore, those within each model should seek in humility to find the genius and

---

8   Ibid., 212-216. Cf. Kevin De Young, "Two Kingdom Theology and Neo-Kuyperians," https://blogs.thegospelcoalition.org/kevindeyoung/2009/08/14/two-kingdom-theology-and-neo-kuyperians.
9   Ibid., 235. Italics in original.

wisdom of the other approaches to better honor God's Word and his will."[10] This does not mean so much a blending of the models as it does a recognition of the model that best suits our gifts and calling—be that evangelism, care for the poor, intellectual engagement, and so forth. We should inhabit the model that best fits our convictions, whose "tool kit best fits our gifts. Once we know our model, we should be able, depending on the cultural seasons and context, to use tools from other kits." [11]

Keller also urges us to remember the difference between the *organized* and *organic* church (or to use Kuyper's language, the church *as institute* and *organism*). He quotes theologian John Bolt, to the effect that:

> *In Kuyper's view, Christians who go out into their various vocations do so neither as direct emissaries of the institutional church nor as mere individual believers.... And political action does not flow directly from structures and authorities of the church, but comes to expression organically in the various spheres of life as believers live out their faith and spirituality that develops and is nurtured in the church's worship and discipline.*[12]

Bolt, incidentally, is a leading North American expert on Kuyper and neo-Calvinism; yet he also identifies himself

---

10 Ibid, 236-37.
11 Ibid., 240.
12 Ibid., 241. Cf. John Bolt, *A Free Church, A Holy Nation: Abraham Kuyper's American Public Theology* (Grand Rapids: Eerdmans, 2000), 428-29. Italics Keller's.

as an advocate of "two kingdoms doctrine," illustrating Keller's point that we can glean insights from the various models. More than that, Bolt understands two kingdoms doctrine as being compatible with Kuyper's view of the church as institute and organism.[13]

Naturally, advocates of each model, with some justification, balk at the critical evaluations made by Keller and others. Keller does recognise that there are differences within each movement and not all criticisms apply to everyone concerned. Moreover, there are those within each movement who acknowledge the validity of some of the criticisms. For instance, a contemporary leader of neo-Calvinism has recognised that "Generally speaking, [neo-Calvinists] are more noted for their intellectual ability and culture-transforming zeal than for their personal godliness or their living relationship with Jesus Christ."[14] Likewise, another has noted the tendency to triumphalism.[15] On the other hand, David VanDrunen, perhaps the leading contemporary advocate of two kingdoms doctrine, in responding to criticisms that this doctrine is dualistic, even docetic, says "Perhaps some versions of the two-kingdoms doctrine have fit such stereotypes. My task... is not to defend everything that has

13 Personal email correspondence, June 8, 2016. David VanDrunen has made the same point in "Abraham Kuyper and the Reformed Natural Law and Two Kingdoms Traditions" in *Calvin Theological Journal* 42 (2007), 295.
14 Albert Wolters, *https://www.cardus.ca/comment/article/282/what-is-to-be-done-toward-a-neocalvinist-agenda/*.
15 Richard J. Mouw, *Uncommon Decency: Christian Civility in an Uncivil World* (Downers Grove, Il: InterVarsity Press, second edition, 2010), 162.

gone by the name 'two kingdoms,' but to expound a two-kingdoms approach that is thoroughly grounded in the story of Scripture and biblical doctrine."[16] Another two kingdoms advocate, Darryl Hart, has been criticized by a sympathetic reviewer for at times pressing the distinction between the two kingdoms to the point of separation. If the historic doctrine "denotes the difference between two ages and two governments," Hart often writes as if the distinction were between "two airtight spheres, one the sphere of faith and religion, and the other the sphere of everyday life."[17]

The neo-Calvinist vision with its call to recognise the lordship of Christ in all of life has obvious appeal. But like all movements, it does not always reflect the strengths of its founder. As D.A. Carson notes in his *Christ and Culture Revisited*, "Kuyperianism is most attractive when Kuyper's personal piety is in play (in exactly the same way that the reforming zeal of Wilberforce is attractive because of his commitment to the gospel and his transparent evangelical piety). When Kuyperianism... becomes the intellectual structure on which we ground our attempts to influence the culture, yet cuts itself loose from, say, the piety of the Heidelberg Confession (*sic*), the price is sudden death."[18] Carson also points

16 VanDrunen, *Living in God's Two Kingdoms*, 14.
17 Matthew Tuininga, "Two Kingdoms Doctrine: What's all the Fuss About?: Part One, http://www.reformation21.org/articles/the-two-kingdoms-doctrine-whats-the-fuss-all-about-part-one.php. September 2012.
18 D.A. Carson, *Christ & Culture Revisited* (Grand Rapids, MI/Cambridge, U.K.: Eerdmans, 2008), 216. See also, William Young, "Historic Calvinism and Neo-Calvinism" in *Reformed Thought: Selected Writings of William Young*, edited by Joel R. Beeke and Ray B. Lanning (Grand

out that significant social reforms have historically been a by-product of spiritual renewal rather than political activism as such.[19]

Abraham Kuyper (1837-1920),
Prime Minister of the Netherlands, 1901-05

While I fully appreciate Kuyper's distinction between the church as institute and organism, another potential weakness in his followers, pointed out by Keller, is a tendency to understate the role of the institutional church as the visible expression of God's kingdom on earth.[20] Along with this goes a preoccupation with social

Rapids, MI: Reformation Heritage Books, 2011): 25-58. Originally published in two parts in the *Westminster Theological Journal* 36, no 1 (Fall 1973), 36, no. 2 (Winter, 1974). Both Carson and Young trace the spiritual decline of neo-Calvinism to Kuyper's doctrine of presumptive regeneration which can (although not necessarily) lead to a social Christianity without concern for personal piety.

19 Carson, op. cit., 152-53.
20 For a discussion of the view that the church is *the* visible expression of God's kingdom on earth, see Edmund P. Clowney, "The Politics of the

transformation here and now that neglects the New Testament model of the church as sojourners travelling through this world to the final consummation (Psalm 39:2; 1 Chronicles 29:15; Philippians 3: 20; Hebrews 11:9-10, 13, 16; 1 Peter 1:1, 2:11), seeking to be preserving salt and light to the nations (Matthew 5:13-14), but as an often persecuted people to whom the kingdom of heaven belongs (Matthew 5:10) and who desire to be with Christ, which is "better by far" (Philippians 1:23). I agree with advocates of the two kingdoms view that the biblical models of political engagement relevant to us today are Daniel and Esther in Babylonian exile.

Kuyper himself, as the Carson quote implies, was a spiritual as well as intellectual, theological and political giant. His devotional book *To Be Near Unto God* bears witness to this.[21] Kuyper's *Lectures on Calvinism*, delivered at Princeton University in 1898, deals mainly with the application of a Reformed worldview to politics, science and art. But it also includes a lecture on "Calvinism and Religion" where he states that "no sphere of human life is conceivable in which religion does not maintain its demands that God shall be praised, that God's ordinances shall be observed, and that every *labora* shall be permeated with its *ora* in fervent and

---

Kingdom," *Westminster Theological Journal* (Spring, 1979): 303-310. See also Clowney's *The Doctrine of the Church* (Philadelphia, PA: Presbyterian and Reformed, 1976) and chapter 9 of *The Church: Contours of Christian Theology* (Downers Grove, ILL: 1995), 187-97.

21   The first of several English editions was published in 1918 by Eerdmans-Sevenesma Co., Grand Rapids, MI.

ceaseless prayer."[22]

Herman Bavinck, Kuyper's successor as Professor of Theology at the Free University in Amsterdam, expressed concern that "it seems we no longer know what sin and grace, guilt and forgiveness, regeneration and conversion are." He wrote this in the context of a preface to a Dutch translation of the biography of the Scottish eighteenth century divines, Ralph and Ebenezer Erskine. Bavinck showed his appreciation of Scottish preaching that descends "to the depth of the human heart, unsparingly removes all covers and pretences used by men to insulate themselves from the holiness of God, and exposes them in their poverty and lowliness before the face of God."[23] This is the kind of preaching under which James Mackay grew up, helping form his character and prepare him for public service.

So where does this locate Lord Mackay? He has said that he finds it difficult to distinguish between the nuances of the positions outlined above. He does not self-consciously operate on the basis of either model. But his concern for

---

22 Abraham Kuyper, *Lectures on Calvinism* (Grand Rapids, MI: Eerdmans, 1931), 53.

23 "Herman Bavinck on Scottish Covenant Theology and Reformed Piety," translated and introduced by Henk van den Belt, *The Bavinck Review* 3 (2012): 174-75. Although Bavinck defended Kuyper's doctrine of presumptive regeneration, he understood and shared the concern that "it seems that there are no unregenerate in the church any longer. It seems as though even when a person has continued living for years in an unconverted state, he still must be considered to be regenerated." Ibid., 165. Cf. Herman Bavinck, *Saved By Grace: The Holy Spirit's Work in Calling and Regeneration*, trans. Nelson D. Kloosterman, ed. J. Mark Beach (Grand Rapids: Reformation Heritage Books, 2008), 4.

personal godliness coupled with his realistic view of what can be accomplished in a fallen political system seem to me to place him closer to the two kingdoms model. In his own words, a Christian in public office "must act according to Christian principles but he is not alone and must be an influence for good so far as he can in dependence on divine grace."[24] His approach to specific issues has left him open to criticism from church leaders and secularists alike. However, his personal integrity and motives have been above question and even his critics have observed him to be "an honourable man... so utterly ingenuous." This is no small achievement for a Christian living and working in two kingdoms.

All too often Christian involvement in politics seems to involve baptising the political agenda of either the right or the left, whereas neither has a monopoly on biblical priorities. Lord Mackay recognises this. He is a religious and political conservative, but as we saw in the quotation with which our review of his life and work began, when he felt the Conservative-led government of the day was treating single mothers unfairly, he led a "wonderful revolt." Faith-based concerns took priority over political loyalties.

Lord Mackay worked in a context that still officially recognises the establishment of the Christian religion, in particular the Church of England and the Church of Scotland in their different understandings of establishment. We

---

24   Personal email correspondence, July 30, 2013.

saw how he attempted to assess the current situation and wondered if it is not still possible to maintain a national recognition of the Christian religion while recognising the rights of those of all faiths and none. While different in theory from the situation that exists in the United States with its disestablishment of the church, Lord Mackay's principal concern that the church be free to promote and proclaim the kingdom of God seems not too much different from the modified version of the *Westminster Confession of Faith* in American Presbyterianism or of the *Belgic Confession* in Reformed circles of the continental tradition.

Turning to the differences between the legal systems in the United Kingdom and United States, Lord Mackay was quoted to the effect that in the United States judges are selected based on their opinions, whereas in the United Kingdom they are selected based on their ability to form an opinion once they have heard all the evidence. He does acknowledge that judges are not entirely immune to the influence of their own previously held opinions, but what the above statement indicates is that when Lord Mackay was in a position to appoint judges in England and Wales, he did so strictly on the basis of ability and not of ideology. Some might see this as a loss of opportunity to influence the judicial landscape, but it surely demonstrates integrity and fairness, two important Christian virtues.

Finally, we saw that a governing principle in Lord Mackay's political life was concern for families and particularly children in situations of conflict and/or poverty. This led him at times to take positions unpopular with both political and religious conservatives. He did not, however, court controversy. His role in both church and state was more that of a mediator than a crusader, although not shying away from controversy when needed. By his consistently godly character and reasoned approach to justice for all, with the protection of religious rights, he continues to be a light in the world, reflecting the spirit of his Master, seeking always to acknowledge God in all his ways — trusting that as he does so, his steps will be made straight and his paths directed throughout life, as they have thus far been. There is much here to be learned by fellow Christians in public office, be they British or American (never more so than now) or of any other nationality.

Appendix 1

This is the speech delivered by Lord Mackay on the second reading of the Family Law Bill in the House of Lords, 30 November 1995. HANSARD 1803–2005 → 1990s → 1995 → November 1995 → 30 November 1995 → Lords Sitting Family Law Bill [H.L.] HL Deb 30 November 1995 vol. 567 cc700-90700. The speech is printed as it appeared in HANSARD.

My Lords, I beg to move that this Bill be now read a second time.

I should like to begin this important debate by reaffirming my commitment and that of the Government to marriage. I personally believe that it is a divinely appointed institution and this Government will not do anything to undermine it.

The provisions of the Bill have been brought before your Lordships against a background of long and detailed debate and consultation, not only about the problems with the present divorce law and how the situation might be improved but also about the need to support marriage.

What has emerged very clearly from the recent debate is a very grave concern about marriage and the need for greater emphasis on and support for marriage. This debate has been as much about marriage as it has been about the finer details of a divorce system. This must be right because we cannot look at marriage and divorce in isolation from each other. The Government firmly believe that they have a role in supporting the services available to help not only those whose marriage is in difficulty but also those considering entering marriage. This is why the Government provide funding to marriage guidance and marriage research organisations.

The Government are, however, concerned that the best use is made of the resources available to support marriage. That is why we have also set up an inter-departmental working group on marriage. This group seeks to identify the needs of couples in relation to preparing for marriage and for guidance and support during marriage; the range of services currently available in this area, the extent to which their existence is known and how this knowledge might be increased; and how existing resources might best be used to meet the needs of couples who are considering marriage or whose marriage is in difficulty.

Under the provisions in Part I of the Family Law Bill, the ground for divorce would remain the irretrievable breakdown of marriage. At present, it is possible to establish breakdown by producing evidence of adultery, behaviour, desertion or separation. None of these requires the conduct in question to have been the cause of the irretrievable breakdown of the marriage. The court's judgment proceeds on the basis that the marriage has broken down irretrievably. At present, therefore, the real reason for the breakdown of marriage may have little to do with the alleged fault which forms the basis of almost 75 per cent of divorce petitions. The law makes no attempt to investigate what really made the marriage break down. This is not the fault of the judges, the courts or the lawyers. In an intimate relationship such as marriage, it is usually very difficult to obtain evidence on which a human tribunal would come to a fair judgment on that question.

It is a mistake to believe that the present law underlines in any way the idea of responsibility by the use of fault in the ground for divorce. In fact the reality is that the only relevance of fault is to obtain a quick divorce, and that seems to me to run quite contrary to the idea that the concept of fault fortifies the institution of marriage. How can it be said that a requirement to make allegations of fault provides the law with an underlying moral base when in fact to commit a wrong—such as adultery—actually means that you can be divorced in less than six months and so be free to marry again? And how can it be said to support marriage that such a person be free to remarry without having first sorted out all the arrangements consequent upon divorce and so fulfilled the obligations and responsibilities undertaken when the parties married and perhaps became parents? These are questions which I have asked myself many, many times. I have tried hard to see how fault can therefore be said to provide a moral basis for marriage. These are questions which I would suggest to your Lordships are worthy of consideration.

Not only do allegations not need to reflect the real cause of the breakdown but they are often exaggerated and usually uncorroborated. This leads to bitterness and resentment on the part of the accused spouse resulting in conflict which poisons the atmosphere and is very damaging to children. Such an atmosphere cannot help a couple consider whether divorce is the right course of action or indeed try to save their marriage. Even if the marriage has broken down irretrievably, how can such an atmosphere help the couple consider the consequences of divorce and make workable arrangements for the future for their children? I see no merit, either moral, intellectual or practical, in retention of the requirement to make allegations of fault in order to establish breakdown and do so quickly.

It is of course vitally important that marriages are not dissolved if they could be saved and therefore important that the mechanism used for testing breakdown is one which we are satisfied will do just that. The provisions in the Bill are that the breakdown would be established by the passage of an absolute period of time without that period being abridged in any circumstances. The provision would require a person wishing to initiate proceedings to attend a compulsory information session before the period of time starts to run which might lead to divorce. This will not only mark the seriousness of the step being taken but also ensure that essential information is conveyed to people contemplating divorce in the most effective way possible. Information provided will include information about the various services available to help people, including marriage guidance, mediation and legal services. I believe that this will be done most objectively and effectively if done by those who provide the services. It will also deal with alternative options to divorce and the consequences of divorce for the parties and their children. Regulations will provide for exceptions to personal attendance—for example, disability—when alternative arrangements will be made for the information to be conveyed. It is not intended to force spouses to attend together and so the victims of abuse will not be in any way at risk as a result of this provision.

The period of time would be commenced by the lodging of a neutral statement. By that I mean a statement which does not make allegations and does not, at that early stage, state that the marriage has already irretrievably broken down and that the maker of the statement wants a divorce. The spouse or spouses making the statement would be required to declare that he, she or they believe the marriage to have broken down and declare that they understand that the purpose of the period which will follow before an application to the court can be made for either a separation or a divorce order, will be for reflection on whether the marriage can be saved and consideration of the arrangements for the future, should divorce be proceeded with.

The general view of those who were consulted by the Law Commission and by the Government, following the issue of our consultation paper, was that a sufficient period of time should elapse in order to demonstrate quite clearly that the marriage had irretrievably broken down. The period should be sufficiently long to give parties a realistic timescale within which to reflect on whether the marriage could be saved but also a realistic time within which the practical questions about children, home and finances could be resolved. The length of time which most respondents favoured was 12 months. Those who work with children pointed out (and this is a thought which I would commend to your Lordships) that although 12 months may not seem long to us, 12 months is a very long time indeed in the childhood of a young child living with uncertainty. Those consultees who work with children considered that, if the divorce process period went on too long, this would be bad for children. A lengthy period would prolong the agony not only for the adults but also the children, which could be damaging. Hardship could be caused by the imposition of a period longer than 12 months.

It probably has to be accepted that there are limits to how much longer the period can be made without causing too much hardship—particularly to children. Do we really want to make things harder for children? Are things not hard enough for those children who are innocent victims of marriage breakdown?

For those who are the victims of violence, the remedies which will be available under Part III of the Bill will be adequate to protect them during the 12-month process.

A very important requirement in the Bill is the requirement that parties decide all arrangements relating to their children, finance and home before a separation or divorce order can be made. This is an important and significant change from the Law Commission's recommendation. In making this change the Government have been influenced by those who responded to their consultation paper who were of the view that parties who marry should discharge their obligations undertaken when they contracted their earlier marriage, and also their responsibilities which they undertook when they became parents, before they become free to remarry. The Bill provides for certain narrow exceptions to the requirement that all arrangements should be decided before divorce, in order to protect vulnerable parties, such as those who are sick, disabled or being prevented from making arrangements by vindictive and obstructive spouses, and also to protect the children of such parties.

I believe that the requirement that everyone should wait a minimum of a year before applying for an order (as opposed to the small numbers who now wait two years or even smaller numbers who wait five years), together with the requirement that all arrangements will have to be decided before divorce, will do far more to reinforce and underline the institution of marriage and its inherent obligations and responsibilities than the present system which allows quick divorce following allegations of fault.

I should emphasise that the current legislation which enables the conduct of each of the parties to be taken into account by the court, where that conduct is such that it would in the opinion of the court be inequitable to disregard it, when making financial provision orders, will stand as it now is in terms of this Bill.

The Bill provides that it will not be possible to commence a process which would lead to divorce within the first year of marriage with the result that it will not be possible for couples to apply for divorce until they have been married for two years. This will act as a brake on couples rushing into and out of marriage again too quickly.

I have also preserved the power for the court to bar a divorce altogether where one party can show that dissolution of the marriage would result in grave financial or other grave hardship. The court will continue to be able to take account of all the circumstances of the case including the conduct of the parties when considering such a bar. However this bar would be available in all cases and not just, as at present, in five-year separation cases and so has the important potential to protect more spouses.

Research since the last major reform of the ground for divorce has shown us the importance of the need to try to reduce conflict in separation and divorce cases in order to reduce at least some of the damage caused to children. We have also, through research, become much more conscious of the need to help parties try to communicate better during the separation and divorce process and encourage them to try to manage conflict so that they can make arrangements for the future which are workable and better for their children. It is clear that the children who do best after divorce are the children whose parents co-operate in the discharge of their parental responsibilities and who reach amicable arrangements for the future of their children. I am most disturbed by the fact that allegations of fault are used in more cases where there are children than where there are not, and that conflict is more prevalent in cases based on intolerable behaviour. In these important respects, namely, the reduction of conflict and improvement of communication, mediation has been shown to be most effective. The position at the moment is that although under the current Legal Aid Act the Legal Aid Board can pay for mediators' reports to be commissioned, it is not possible for the board to pay for the process of mediation itself, although it is possible for lawyers to be paid for.

I would like this to change. I believe that mediation has enormous potential in appropriate cases and Part II of the Bill therefore provides for the Legal Aid Act to be amended to allow parties who are eligible to apply for state funding for the use of mediation. I am not intending that mediation should become compulsory—compulsory mediation quite simply does not work, and is a contradiction in terms. State funded legal advice and assistance will be available in support of mediation when needed by eligible parties. Legal representation will be available for eligible parties when mediation is not suitable for the parties or appropriate for the circumstances of the case.

In presenting the provisions of Parts I and II of this Bill to the House, I do so against a background of long, detailed and most careful consultation and as a person, as I said at the outset, who has a strong belief in the institution of marriage. I personally believe that marriage should be for life. This is the ideal I believe most couples who marry strive for. It is this ideal which provides the most stable and secure background for the birth and development of children. I personally would not wish to see people divorced at all. I would prefer that spouses remained united until "God separates them by death". But I have to recognise that marriages do break down and that the civil legislator must take account of this fact and provide the best framework of law to cater for this. I believe that according to St. Mark's Gospel (Chapter 10, verses 4 and 5 when Jesus reminds the Pharisees that Moses allowed men to "put away" their wives because of their "hardness of heart", he was referring to a civil legislative system with which they were familiar. I believe also that our Lord's teaching contemplated a civil system in which it would be possible to do what He told His questioners should not he done.

I turn now to Part III of the Bill, which deals with domestic violence and the occupation of the family home. The provisions in this part reform the various remedies which exist in family law to deal with two separate but linked problems. These are: providing protection for one family member from violence or molestation from another family member; and regulating the occupation of the family home where a relationship has broken down, either temporarily or permanently. The Bill will provide a single consistent set of remedies through two types of orders, "non-molestation" orders and "occupation orders". Eligibility for the orders is based on the concept of "association" by way of certain family or domestic connections or through family proceedings. Eligibility for specific orders is further distinguished in the Bill, and depends on the existing property rights of the applicants, as well as their relationship to each other.

This part of the Bill was substantially before your Lordships' House last Session, in the form of the Family Homes and Domestic Violence Bill. It was discussed at great length then in a Special Public Bill Committee and completed all of its stages here before going on to be debated in another place.

For that reason, and because time is limited, I propose to speak now only on the changes that have been made since the Bill was last before your Lordships. At a late stage and just before Prorogation the Bill attracted some controversy. This was based on a belief, I think misconceived, that cohabitants were being placed on an equal footing with married couples for the first time, and that this undermined the institution of marriage.

Although I do not think that the Bill would have had the effect feared, I accept that there is genuine concern to uphold the special nature of marriage. This is a concern I share, and for that reason I have made four changes to the Bill that was before this House in the last Session.

First, I have introduced a general clause on marriage. This instructs the courts to have regard, when making an occupation order for a cohabitant, to the fact that they have chosen not to give each other the commitment that a married couple have chosen to give. I hope that this will emphasise the important general message that marriage is special in a way that no other relationship is.

Secondly, the previous Bill made provision for the procedure for resolving property disputes contained in the Married Women's Property Act to be available to cohabitants. I have removed that provision. Although the extension was purely of procedure it was the subject of specific concern, and I think it is right to respond to those concerns.

Thirdly, concern was expressed about a cohabitant who had no right to occupy a property gaining long-term possession of it. For this reason I have now provided that in such circumstances an order, which may be for a maximum of six months (that was the old provision), may be extended only once. It was possible under the former provision to extend it again and again, indefinitely. This contrasts with the position for spouses and ex-spouses. I believe this further distinguishes between marriage and cohabitation and still retains the essential of what is required.

Fourthly, it was possible under the old Bill for the court in certain circumstances to be under a duty to make an occupation order in favour of a cohabitant with no right to occupy the home. This duty came about by the operation of the "balance of harm" test, as it was called. In these cases I have recast the test in such a way that there is no duty on the court to make such an order, but simply a discretionary power to permit it to do so. The court can have regard in considering that matter to all the circumstances of the case.

I believe that the overall effect of these amendments is to emphasise the difference between marriage and cohabitation while at the same time providing protection where it is needed. Marriage is a lifetime commitment, publicly entered into. It gives the parties to the marriage rights and obligations to each other which can continue even after the marriage has ended. Cohabitation is not the same. Although individual cohabitants may intend their relationship to continue indefinitely, they do not have the same obligations to one another or the same rights as married partners. It is important that the law provides protection against domestic violence for those who need it. But I also believe that a distinction between marriage and cohabitation can and should be drawn. I believe that Part III of the Bill does that. I ask your Lordships for support for the changes that I have made in an attempt to reach consensus on this matter.

This is an important Bill which deals with areas fundamental to people's lives. I feel that it is right that Parliament should have an opportunity of considering this matter in a Bill promoted by the Government in government time. After prolonged thought, I have put forward what I consider are the best proposals. I am happy to see them improved, if Parliament can suggest improvements. I hope that we can all approach this matter in a spirit of united resolve to do the best that we can for families in England and Wales in the years to come. I commend the Bill to the House.

Moved, That the Bill be now read a second time.

Appendix 2

Does Establishment Have a Future?

On 9 May, 2013, Lord Mackay delivered the Richard O'Sullivan Memorial Lecture, on behalf of Theos *and* Law and Justice: the Christian Law Review. *The text of the lecture follows, reprinted with kind permission from* Theos: Clear thinking on religion and society, *13 May, 2013.*

Who was Richard O'Sullivan in whose honour this Lecture was founded?

He was a barrister who was born in Cork, and practised for many years at the Bar, being a member of Middle Temple of which he was Treasurer in 1960-1. He took silk in 1934, and became Recorder of Derby.

He was interested in the Christian origins of the common law and wrote widely on this subject, and also founded the Thomas More Society to bring together Catholic lawyers and others. Papers delivered to the Society were published, to which he contributed. Today he might well have become an academic.

He set himself to expound the theological origins of English law, and brought out its theological roots in the work of men who were both priests and lawyers, like Bracton. In particular, he put forward the concept of the 'free and lawful man' - 'liber et legalis homo'; and also drew on the Christian sense of the equality of human nature, and argued that this Christian sense of human equality has passed into the texture of English thought and language. He felt strongly that the common law started with the presumption that men (women now too of course) were reasonable beings, endowed with reason by the law of nature, and so this presumption should be carried forward to the law today.

When this journal, Law and Justice, was founded in 1963 he had recently died and was well known in Catholic legal circles, which is why the Trust decided to sponsor a lecture in his memory. They are actually thinking of publishing a selection of his papers.

Incidentally, the journal began with a Roman Catholic emphasis, but long ago broadened out to look at the whole area of Christian engagement with the law.

Some previous lecturers have been Lords Hailsham, Scarman and Nolan. A high standard has been set. It will be for you to judge whether it has been attained today.

When John Duddington wrote to invite me to give this lecture, I did not immediately leap to accept. I felt the title contained a challenge to prophesy. I have never felt very secure in attempting to foretell the future. The more I thought about it the more I realised that the challenge was more to analyse the present in the light of the past, and the developments in the relation between Church and State in the two nations where I had some acquaintance with these matters.

I should make it clear at the outset that I understand the word "establishment" in the title set for me as meaning the present relationship between the Church of England and the State.

Though there is much in the Old Testament that has a bearing on this subject, I shall begin with the setting up of the Christian Church by our Lord himself in what has often been described as the Great Commission, when he said to his disciples when He was about to go from them:

All power is given unto me in heaven and in earth. Go ye therefore, and teach all nations, baptizing them in the name of the Father, and of the Son, and of the Holy Ghost; Teaching them to observe all things whatsoever I have commanded you: and, lo, I am with you alway, even unto the end of the world. (Matthew 28: 18b-20)

Some simple points emerge from this charter of the Church. First, Jesus spoke of the nations as then existing to be the subject of the disciples' efforts. Second, He asked his disciples to teach the nations his commandments and to baptise. There is no reference to the disciples ruling the nations. Third, as the holder of all power He is to be with his disciples until the end of the world, and that implies that as they taught the nations they did so with His authority.

It is also worthy of note that when Pilate asked Jesus whether He was King of the Jews, Jesus explained that His kingdom was not of this world (John 18:36). It may be worth pointing out that in Christian history the question has regularly been asked, what this statement of Jesus has to say about the relationship of those who recognise Jesus' lordship to civil governments and the means of power they use. As the distinguished New Testament commentator Herman Ridderbos points out, "the passage does not in fact discuss this question." Far from portraying "a confrontation of Jesus' kingdom with the state," Jesus' words rather indicate "that his kingdom is distinct from 'the kingdom of this world' at a point of immediate interest: it is not based on force". This rejection of defence by violence during his arrest does not, states Ridderbos, constrain the conclusion that Jesus "would also demand the total defencelessness of his disciples in times of oppression and that he would reject all use of worldly power for their benefit as incompatible with his kingdom."

As the disciples went on the mission on which Jesus sent them, they suffered a great deal at the hands of the rulers of the nations to whom they went but, in spite of the opposition, the Church grew until eventually it was embraced by the Emperor Constantine as the religion of the Empire: an early example of its establishment.

As the years rolled on and the Church became more powerful, it manifested considerable muscle, particularly in the nations that came to be known as Christendom. Although it experienced the great division between the Eastern and the Western Churches, particularly in the West, it continued to make vassals of nations and their rulers, and to dominate law and order until the Reformation.

We are all familiar with what happened in England where what has been called the King's Reformation occurred. As a result of Henry VIII 's desire for a male heir, and the Pope's refusal to let him divorce Catherine of Aragon, Henry decided that he would himself take over from the Pope as head of the church in England. No change in the tenets of the church was involved, except those concerned with the government of the church. Thus it became true that the Monarch became "in all causes ecclesiastical as well as civil throughout his realms supreme," and the title of Defender of the Faith that the Pope had earlier conferred on Henry remained appropriate, since the change affected only the government of the church and not the faith which it confessed.

It is clear that Henry's object was to gain control of the church so that he would gain the Church's authority to divorce Catherine. I have seen it suggested that there was a desire for change on other grounds among the people of England.

Since that time the relationship has been subject to many

changes. The principal features of the relationship today are that Her Majesty the Queen, as our ruling monarch, is the Supreme Governor of the Church of England. Parliament has certain authority over the Church, although the Church has power to regulate its worship, subject to a condition I will mention later. The Crown has the power of appointment to many offices in the Church; twenty six bishops of the Church of England have seats in the House of Lords; the Church of England clergy conduct national services in England such as the Coronation, royal marriages, celebration of royal anniversaries and national anniversaries such as the armistice day at the Cenotaph; and the Archbishop of Canterbury, as a matter of protocol, has precedence immediately after the Royal Family.

It is worthy of note that the Succession to the Crown Act, recently passed, does not alter the unambiguous provisions of the Bill of Rights and the Act of Settlement requiring the Sovereign to be a Protestant and in communion with the Church of England.

The Church of England has power to legislate by means of Measures to alter the laws affecting it. These are laid before a special Committee of members of both Houses of Parliament, called the Ecclesiastical Committee, for consideration. If thereafter a Measure is approved by each House by resolution, it goes forward for Royal Assent and, on that being given, it becomes law as if it were an Act of Parliament.

By virtue of the Church of England (Worship and Doctrine) Measure 1974, the Church has power by Canon to alter the Worship of the Church if the doctrine of the Church is not adversely affected. References in the Measure to the doctrine of the Church of England are to be construed in accordance with the following statement:

The doctrine of the Church of England is grounded in the Holy Scriptures, and in such teachings of the ancient Fathers and Councils as are agreeable to the said Scriptures. In particular such doctrine is to be found in the Thirty-nine Articles of Religion, the Book of Common Prayer, and the Ordinal.

My reading of the Measure is that the Church itself is the judge of whether the doctrinal condition is breached. The Measure thus removes the difficulty at the root of the 1928 controversy relating to the change of the Prayer Book. On that occasion Winston Churchill warned that by defeating the proposal again, the House of Commons "would inaugurate a period of chaos which could only be corrected by disestablishment." You can see why I am reluctant to embark on prophecy.

What are the challenges this relationship faces today?

Firstly, and as the general context of the current debate, since the 1960s there has been growing opposition from the secularist lobby to the establishment of the church. The secularist position represents a commitment to a relativistic approach to religious truth, and therefore holds that the Christian faith should abandon its claim to be in possession of absolute or final truth. This, together with the assumption of a radical split between the public realm of "facts" and the private realm of "values" (religion finding its place entirely within the private domain), means, as pointed out by the late great missionary statesman and ecumenist Bishop Lesslie Newbigin, that "the rival truth claims of the different religions are not felt to call for argument or resolution; they are simply part of the mosaic – or perhaps one should say kaleidoscope – of different values that make up the whole pattern." Since all religions are equal in status and independently valid, the secularist argument goes, it is inappropriate for any particular religion to enjoy the privilege of establishment.

As Bishop Newbigin states, however, "no state can be completely secular in the sense that those who exercise power have no beliefs about what is true and no commitment to what they believe to be right." It is sometimes forgotten that the position of ideological pluralism, espoused by secularism, itself involves a claim to absolute truth, affirming as it does, in the words of a distinguished Biblical scholar and theologian, "the dogmatic opinion that all dogmatic opinions are to be ruled out." [Prof. D.A. Carson] Or, as Newbigin puts it, "The difference is not between those who rely on dogma and those who don't. It's the difference between those who know what the dogma is they are relying on, and those who do not."

True tolerance does not imply indifference to the truth. In a society which has been nourished in its deepest roots by the Christian faith and tradition, can it really be impossible to envisage, with Newbigin, "a state that acknowledges the Christian faith as true, but deliberately provides full security for those of other views"?

Philip Collins, writing in the *Times* on 28 December 2012 said: "A multicultural nation is poorly symbolised by the establishment of one faith." He also refers to the falling attendance on Church of England services as a support to this argument. There is no doubt that on great national and anniversary occasions many do attend, either in person or via the media, services led by the Church of England, and that in areas of religious and ethical division an office-holder in the Church of England, often the local bishop, is regarded as the leader of meetings to dissipate tensions.

At the beginning of the Diamond Jubilee celebrations, Her Majesty the Queen attended a function at the Archbishop of Canterbury's London home, when she said this:

Here at Lambeth Palace we should remind ourselves of the significant position of the Church of England in our nation's life. The concept of our established Church is occasionally misunderstood and, I believe, commonly under-appreciated. Its role is not to defend Anglicanism to the exclusion of other religions. Instead the Church has a duty to protect the free practice of all faiths in this country.

I should also mention the fact that 26 Bishops have seats in the House of Lords, as an aspect of this particular challenge. It has to be kept in mind that the role of the House of Lords in legislating is subservient to that of the House of Commons, and that no provision can form part of an Act of Parliament without the consent of the House of Commons, and no such provision can be prevented from becoming such a part, except for a delay of one year, if the House of Commons agrees that it should. I think it can be said that the bishops see their role in the Lords as according with Her Majesty's statement, and to bring the attention of the House to Christian principles bearing on matters under discussion.

It is certainly not the case that all adherents of non-Christian faiths in Britain view themselves as ill-served by the establishment of one faith. Terry Sanderson, president of the National Secular Society quotes, with disapproval, the view of the Chief Rabbi, Lord Jonathan Sacks, as reported by Archbishop John Sentamu on the BBC Radio 4 Today programme, that one benefit of establishment is that "it keeps religion at the forefront of the nation." There is some evidence that the Chief Rabbi's view of establishment may be quite widely shared by people belonging to diverse faith groups.

Secondly, it is sometimes held that this relationship is one that necessarily impedes the mission of the church, as set out in the terms of our Lord's Great Commission to which reference was earlier made.

Let me offer two particularly colourful examples. The first was elegantly expressed in 1968 by the late Professor D M Mackinnon, a distinguished Scottish Episcopalian, who was Professor of Divinity in the University of Cambridge. "Where England is concerned, the passing of Establishment as we have known it would surely lead to a day in which episcopal lawn sleeves would cease to flutter in the breeze as their wearer bestowed the diocesan benediction upon the latest Polaris submarine". Philip Collins, writing in the Times on 28 December 2012, is equally graphic: "It is easy for church ministers to avert their eyes from the dismal truth if invitations to fancy - dress state balls drop regularly on to the rectory doormat."

In different ways, these both express the view that ministers of the gospel are at risk of not being faithful to their Divine Master if they serve in a church that has a state connection. Whatever walk of life we follow, we will face risk of being lured from loyalty to our Lord's teaching by some distraction. Our Lord Jesus understood our vulnerability in this respect and also the way we should handle it when He taught us to pray, "Lead us not into temptation." The vigorous criticism of Government policy from the standpoint of Christian principles, emanating from the highest levels in the Church of England in recent years, seems evidence that this prayer in the Church has been made and answered. However I do not underestimate the continual danger of this threat.

My impression is that a closely related threat arises from the wish to be popular or acceptable to public opinion. This is not, in my view, the result of establishment. We all must be conscious of this whatever church we support, established or disestablished, or if in our lives we are guided by moral principles which may have no religious base. There is always a possibility that the generally held view will differ from ours. Are we to go along with the tide or stick to our principles? It is usually easier to go along with the tide. Swimming against it involves strength of commitment. In his tribute to Baroness Thatcher, Lord Tebbit remarked that, "She pursued that which she believed to be right. I must say that as her party chairman I found that my life was made much easier by my understanding of the certainties of her beliefs. She never asked me to commission a focus group."

So far as the Church is concerned, its duty is to follow its Commission and to teach the nation what it has received from its Master. That is the source of its authority. The scriptures and post biblical history contain many examples where the Church's message has not been popular, but I do not see that its being established is of itself an impediment to the Church's mission.

Frequently alleged also, it should be said, is the threat of interference by Parliament in the affairs of the Church. As I have narrated above, developments in the relationship between Parliament and the Church over the years have greatly reduced this possibility. The proposals of the Government on same sex marriage have made clear that it is not intended to require the Church of England to act upon these. This, I think, tends to confirm this trend.

It is often argued that the place of the Christian and the Church must necessarily be outwith all established power, in the place of the victim and protestor. It is of course true that in the light of the cross "no political order can be identified with the reign of God." It is nevertheless a mistake to see Jesus simply, as Newbigin said, as "the greatest of those who have died in revolt against established power."

Rather, "Jesus died as the beloved Son of the Father, by whom the powers that killed him are authorised." What Jesus condemned was not Pilate's authority but its abuse. As Newbigin says:

All kingship from Calvary onwards is tested and judged by the standard of the true kingship established there; judged and tested, not eliminated.

As Jesus exercised his kingship by bearing witness to the truth, so the church, as an essential part of its mission, is called to seek to shape public life in the light of Christian truth.

The necessary distinction between (church and state) with respect to their powers and responsibilities does not negate the fact that those who exercise political authority are responsible to God – the only God, Father, Son, and Holy Spirit – and it is the duty of the church to remind them in season and out of season of that fact.

Since both church and state receive their mandate from the God who is revealed in Christ, the provision of Establishment may be seen as providing valuable, God-given, opportunities in furthering the church's vital task of bearing witness to the supreme kingship of Jesus before the principalities and powers of this present age.

John has also asked me to sketch the development of relations between Church and State in Scotland and I now turn to do that. Some humility in doing so is appropriate, as the Bishop of Durham is reported to have said in 1930, "The principal factor in the Church of Scotland's successful achievement of autonomy in establishment is the political insignificance of Scotland. Who cares what is done or said in the Scottish Churches?" It is interesting to note that one of his successors demitted that office to take up office in the University of St Andrews.

In Scotland, the authority of the Roman Catholic Church and the Pope were renounced by what has been called the Reformation Parliament, in 1560. The constitutional position of the church was described in an exchange between Andrew Melville and King James VI of Scotland in 1596, when Melville told the King that there were two kings and two kingdoms in Scotland, and one was "Christ

Jesus the King and his kingdom the Kirk, whose subject King James the Sixth is, and of whose kingdom he is not a king, nor a lord, nor a head, but a member."

I pass over the consequences of this exchange and note that at the ratification of the Treaty of Union between England and Scotland in 1707 it was provided that the Church of Scotland was to remain the true Protestant religion, and the worship, discipline and government of this Church were to remain without any alteration to the people of Scotland in all generations. In 1712 Parliament passed the Church Patronage Act, with profound consequences. In the first half of the 19th century, a series of cases in the courts brought to a head the dispute about who should choose the minister of a congregation, the patron under the Act of Parliament, or the members of the congregation. The courts decided in favour of the patron, and as a result a very substantial number of the ministers and people left the Church of Scotland, one of the leaders of the Disruption, Thomas Chalmers, declaring that they had left a vitiated establishment, but would be happy to return to a pure one.

The new Church was the Church of Scotland Free or as it came to be known as the Free Church of Scotland. This Church was set up as a church independent of the state, but holding as part of its doctrine to the establishment principle. That principle had been stated in the Westminster Confession, approved by the General Assembly of the Church of Scotland in 1647 and approved by the Scottish

Parliament in 1649, and again in 1690, and is described in this way in a decision of the House of Lords when the constitution of the Free Church of Scotland was under discussion: "It is the duty of the civil magistrate to maintain and support an establishment of religion in accordance with God's Word."

In 1900 the Free Church of Scotland united with the United Presbyterian Church of Scotland to form the United Free Church of Scotland. The United Presbyterian Church was composed of successors to people who had left the Church of Scotland earlier, on doctrinal grounds, and who did not accept the establishment principle. A small number of ministers and elders of the Free Church refused to join the union. Hence the litigation to which I earlier referred, in which they claimed the property of the Free Church on the ground that the united Church did not subscribe to principles of the Free Church on which the title to its property depended. The United Church lost the litigation, but since the numbers of those who did not join the union were so small that they could not hope to use the property to which they had been found entitled, the Royal Commission was set up to divide the property on a practical basis. In due course negotiations were initiated for the re-union of the United Free Church with the Church of Scotland and, as a precursor to such union, the Church of Scotland Act 1921 was passed, which made it clear that no civic authority had power to legislate or to adjudicate finally on any matter of doctrine, worship, government and discipline in the church.

The relationship with the civil magistrate is defined in the Schedule to that Act as follows;

VI *This Church acknowledges the divine appointment and authority of the civil magistrate within his own sphere, and maintains its historic testimony to the duty of the nation acting in its corporate capacity to render homage to God, to acknowledge the Lord Jesus Christ to be King over the nations, to obey His laws, to reverence His ordinances, to honour His Church, and to promote in all appropriate ways the Kingdom of God. The Church and the State owe mutual duties to each other, and acting within their respective spheres may signally promote each other's welfare. The Church and the State have the right to determine each for itself all questions concerning the extent and the continuance of their mutual relations in the discharge of these duties and the obligations arising therefrom.*

The re-union finally took place in 1929. The Church of Scotland has enjoyed financial autonomy since 1933. Her Majesty, the Queen appoints a person, the Lord High Commissioner to represent her at the General Assembly if she does not attend Herself. The Moderator invites him or her to address the Assembly near the beginning of the meeting, and near the end, but he or she does not intervene in any other way.

I think it can be said that the relationship of the State

to the Church of Scotland is one of recognition with a degree of support. As Professor Frank Lyall has said, "All that establishment means is that the civil authority has recognised the Church's self-imposed task to bring the ordinances of religion to all Scotland, and looks to the Church on suitable ceremonial occasions." If Scotland were to become a separate State from the rest of the United Kingdom, I would expect the relationship between the State and the Church of Scotland would remain the same.

The relationship between the State and the Church of England could be described as one of limited participation of the State in the Church of England.

The Church of Ireland was disestablished by the Irish Church Act 1869 which took effect on 1 January 1871. The Church in Wales was disestablished by the Welsh Church Act 1914 which came into force in 1920.

The relationship of the State to the Church which carries the name of the country in which it functions differs markedly from place to place but I conclude by saying that I believe the promise with which I started, namely, that the Church, whatever her vicissitudes, and whatever her relationship with the State, will enjoy the presence of her Master who founded her, when she is carrying out His Commission.

Photo by Karen Huttenga, courtesy of *The Banner*

J. Cameron Fraser was born in Zimbabwe and grew up in Scotland. After graduating from the University of Edinburgh, he studied at Westminster Theological Seminary (Philadelphia), and later received a D.Min. degree from Trinity Evangelical Divinity School. Following thirty years of pastoral ministry in western Canada, he now serves the Southern Alberta and Saskatchewan congregations of the Christian Reformed Church in various ways that include administration (as stated clerk), preaching and mentoring. He also works part-time with Streets Alive Mission in Lethbridge, Alberta. A former magazine editor, Cameron has authored or co-authored four previous books. He is married with two adult sons and four granddaughters.

CPSIA information can be obtained
at www.ICGtesting.com
Printed in the USA
BVOW06s1128230817
492884BV00014B/201/P